The History of Mexico

CRAFTED BY SKRIUWER

Copyright © 2025 by Skriuwer.

All rights reserved. No part of this book may be used or reproduced in any form whatsoever without written permission except in the case of brief quotations in critical articles or reviews.

At **Skriuwer**, we're more than just a team—we're a global community of people who love books. In Frisian, "Skriuwer" means "writer," and that's at the heart of what we do: creating and sharing books with readers worldwide. Wherever you are in the world, **Skriuwer** is here to inspire learning.

Frisian is one of the oldest languages in Europe, closely related to English and Dutch, and is spoken by about **500,000 people** in the province of **Friesland** (Fryslân), located in the northern Netherlands. It's the second official language of the Netherlands, but like many minority languages, Frisian faces the challenge of survival in a modern, globalized world.

We're using the money we earn to promote the Frisian language.

For more information, contact : **kontakt@skriuwer.com** (www.skriuwer.com)

Disclaimer:
The images in this book are creative reinterpretations of historical scenes. While every effort was made to accurately capture the essence of the periods depicted, some illustrations may include artistic embellishments or approximations. They are intended to evoke the atmosphere and spirit of the times rather than serve as precise historical records.

TABLE OF CONTENTS

CHAPTER 1: MESOAMERICAN BEGINNINGS

- Earliest migration routes and settlements
- Transition from nomadic to agricultural societies
- Foundations for later Mesoamerican cultures

CHAPTER 2: THE RISE OF THE OLMECS

- Geographic and environmental setting along the Gulf Coast
- Social and political organization under elite rulers
- Artistic achievements, colossal heads, and cultural legacy

CHAPTER 3: THE ZAPOTECS AND MONTE ALBÁN

- Origins in the Oaxaca Valley
- City planning and monumental architecture
- Religion, society, and early writing systems

CHAPTER 4: TEOTIHUACAN: THE CITY OF THE GODS

- Urban development and the rise of a major trade hub
- Pyramids of the Sun and Moon, and ceremonial centers
- Social structure and religious practices

CHAPTER 5: THE CLASSIC MAYA

- Flourishing city-states in the tropical lowlands
- Achievements in writing, astronomy, and mathematics
- Socio-political organization and the role of dynastic rulers

CHAPTER 6: THE TOLTECS AND TULA

- Emergence in central Mexico after Teotihuacan's decline
- Influence on art and architecture (Atlantean figures)
- Connections to later Aztec legends and mythologies

CHAPTER 7: THE MIXTECS AND POST-CLASSIC OAXACA

- Migration and settlement in highland Oaxaca
- Codices, art styles, and ruling dynasties
- Role in regional power struggles

CHAPTER 8: THE RISE OF THE AZTECS

- Origins and journey to the Basin of Mexico
- Foundation of Tenochtitlán
- Early alliances and military expansion

CHAPTER 9: AZTEC SOCIETY AND BELIEFS

- Complex class structure, markets, and daily life
- Pantheon of gods, rituals, and the importance of sacrifice
- Education, arts, and cultural values

CHAPTER 10: THE SPANISH ARRIVE

- European explorers and the first encounters
- Impact of diseases and new weapons
- Early alliances with indigenous groups

CHAPTER 11: THE CONQUEST OF TENOCHTITLÁN

- *Hernán Cortés and the march to the Aztec capital*
- *Siege warfare, alliances, and eventual fall of the city*
- *Consequences for the Mesoamerican world*

CHAPTER 12: EARLY COLONIAL RULE

- *Establishment of New Spain*
- *Encomienda system and social hierarchy*
- *Administration and governance under the Spanish Crown*

CHAPTER 13: THE CHURCH AND SOCIETY IN COLONIAL MEXICO

- *Catholic missions and conversion efforts*
- *Role of the clergy in education and health*
- *Influence of religious orders on local culture*

CHAPTER 14: ECONOMIC FOUNDATIONS OF NEW SPAIN

- *Silver mining, agriculture, and transatlantic trade*
- *Labor systems and exploitation of native populations*
- *Urban centers and mercantile networks*

CHAPTER 15: ENLIGHTENMENT AND REFORM

- *Spread of Enlightenment ideas in the colony*
- *Bourbon Reforms and administrative changes*
- *Growing discontent among different social classes*

CHAPTER 16: THE INDEPENDENCE MOVEMENT

- Early uprisings and key figures (Hidalgo, Morelos)
- Social and political motivations for rebellion
- Prolonged warfare and eventual victory

CHAPTER 17: THE EARLY REPUBLIC

- Formation of a new government
- Political conflicts and regional power struggles
- Efforts to unify diverse territories

CHAPTER 18: FOREIGN INTERVENTIONS

- Conflicts with European powers
- Loss of territories and national identity crises
- Impact on economic and political stability

CHAPTER 19: THE ROAD TO THE REVOLUTION

- Social inequality and peasant unrest
- Rise of political opposition and revolutionary leaders
- Significance of rural revolts in shaping rebellion

CHAPTER 20: THE MEXICAN REVOLUTION AND ITS AFTERMATH

- Major battles and personalities (Zapata, Villa, Carranza)
- Restructuring of power and society
- Long-term effects on modern Mexican identity

CHAPTER 1

Mesoamerican Beginnings (circa 15,000 BCE – 2000 BCE)

Mexico's history starts with the earliest human presence in what we now call Mesoamerica. This chapter explores how ancient peoples arrived, how they survived, and how they laid the groundwork for the great civilizations yet to come. We begin with migratory groups crossing into the region, then move to the Archaic period, during which people shifted from constant movement to more settled communities.

1.1 Early Migration and Settlement

During the last Ice Age, small groups of nomadic hunters are believed to have crossed from Asia to North America via the Bering Land Bridge. Over generations, they moved south, encountering different climates and landscapes. In central and southern Mexico, they found diverse environments, from deserts to thick forests.

These early people hunted large animals like mammoths and bison, using stone tools crafted for specific tasks. As the climate warmed, big game became scarce. People adapted by hunting smaller animals and gathering wild plants. This lifestyle persisted for thousands of years, forming the basis of early cultures in Mesoamerica.

1.2 Transition to the Archaic Period

Around 8000 BCE to 2000 BCE, the Archaic period saw gradual movement from nomadic ways toward settled living. People discovered that planting seeds like wild squash or maize near camps guaranteed a more reliable food source. This led to the beginnings of agriculture, though it happened slowly.

Domestication of Maize
One of the major developments was the domestication of maize from a wild grass called teosinte. Early farmers selected seeds from plants with larger kernels. Over many generations, this process produced cobs with more edible kernels, an enormous shift in food supply. Squash, beans, and chili peppers were also cultivated alongside maize.

Even as some people started farming, they still hunted and gathered to fill in the gaps. Over time, however, more reliable farming methods allowed villages to form and grow.

Housing and Social Changes
These early villages consisted of simple huts, often made of sticks or reeds, providing shelter from the elements. Families shared tasks like tending crops or hunting. With more stable food sources, some individuals focused on new skills, such as pottery-making. This era also saw early religious practices, as people developed rituals to honor their ancestors and the forces of nature that sustained them.

1.3 Cultural Developments and Regional Diversity

As these communities spread, they adapted to local conditions. In highland areas, the climate was cooler, while coastal lowlands were warm and humid. Each group developed unique ways to farm, hunt, and worship. Archaeological evidence suggests religious practices that centered on nature and animal spirits, reflecting a deep connection to the land.

Early Rituals and Beliefs
Without a formal writing system, we rely on artifacts and structures to learn about their beliefs. Cave sites or mountaintops may have been sacred places. Simple offerings or carved stones indicate early forms of spiritual life that foreshadowed the grand temples of later societies.

Trade and Exchange
Even during these formative times, groups traded goods like shells, obsidian, and other raw materials. Through this trading, knowledge about farming or pottery styles could spread. This exchange fostered cultural interaction across the region.

1.4 Archaeological Evidence and Key Sites

Archaeologists study remnants of tools, fire pits, and early dwellings to piece together these ancient lifeways. Important sites include:

- **Tlapacoya (near modern Mexico City):** Stone tools and bones hint at organized hunting parties.
- **Tehuacán Valley (Puebla):** Known for early maize cultivation.
- **Guila Naquitz Cave (Oaxaca):** Evidence of squash and other plant domestication.

Carbon dating and other methods help establish timelines for these discoveries. By examining layers of soil and the artifacts within them, researchers reconstruct how people lived and evolved over centuries.

1.5 The Significance of Early Mesoamerican Roots

This period set the stage for everything that followed. As farming grew more reliable, communities grew larger and more complex. This led to increasingly intricate social structures, religious ideas, and art forms. Variations in climate and geography also produced cultural diversity, with groups adapting to highlands, coasts, and jungles.

Over time, some of these groups merged or were displaced, while others gained power and influence. But at this early stage, the key developments—agriculture, settlement, and basic religious practices—were already in place.

1.6 Transition to Early Complex Societies

By about 2000 BCE, many villages in Mesoamerica had grown in size and organization. Families that controlled farming resources or religious rituals became more influential, and skilled craftspeople produced pottery, textiles, and tools.

In the next chapter, we look at the Olmecs, often called Mesoamerica's "Mother Culture." They built large ceremonial centers and developed a distinctive art style. Their achievements in sculpture, urban planning, and trade networks greatly influenced later civilizations like the Maya and Aztecs.

CHAPTER 2

The Rise of the Olmecs (circa 1500 BCE – 400 BCE)

This chapter focuses on the Olmecs, who lived along the Gulf Coast of Mexico in what are now parts of Veracruz and Tabasco. They are famed for their colossal stone heads, intricate religious symbols, and monumental architecture. Considered by some as the "Mother Culture" of Mesoamerica, the Olmecs left a deep cultural footprint on the region.

2.1 Geographic and Environmental Setting

The Olmec heartland was hot, humid, and filled with rivers and marshy lowlands. Despite challenges like frequent floods, the land was rich in natural resources. Rivers provided fish, transportation routes, and fertile floodplains for farming.

Resource Utilization
Olmecs farmed maize, beans, and squash, while also harvesting local plants and hunting game such as deer. Trade items like rubber, salt, and cacao passed through their territory, boosting their influence.

Climatic Challenges
Managing swampy terrain required ingenuity. Drainage systems and raised platforms helped protect ceremonial centers from floods, reflecting advanced planning and organization.

2.2 Key Olmec Sites

San Lorenzo
Flourishing around 1200 BCE, San Lorenzo featured massive earthworks and advanced drainage systems. Archaeologists have found basalt heads weighing several tons, hinting at the labor and skill involved in transporting and carving them.

La Venta
Rising after San Lorenzo's decline, La Venta became a major Olmec center between 900 BCE and 400 BCE. Its Great Pyramid and ceremonial complexes

contained precious offerings like jade figurines and mosaic pavements. These suggest strong religious and political structures led by elites.

Tres Zapotes
Known for artifacts dating to around 600 BCE, Tres Zapotes carried on Olmec traditions while also displaying cultural shifts. Stela C here features an early Long Count date, indicating that calendar systems in Mesoamerica may have roots in Olmec times.

2.3 Social and Political Organization

Evidence suggests the Olmecs had a stratified society, where rulers or priests directed construction projects and religious rites. Elite figures lived in central areas, coordinating labor for building ceremonial centers.

Urban Planning and Labor
Creating earthen platforms, pyramids, and other infrastructure required significant manpower. Leaders likely commanded laborers to quarry stones, transport them, and shape them into monuments.

Role of Religion
Religion shaped Olmec life. Colossal heads and carved altars, often depicting supernatural motifs, likely served religious or political functions. Priests led

rituals to connect with gods or ancestral spirits, possibly involving ceremonial offerings or bloodletting.

2.4 Olmec Art and Iconography

Olmec art stands out for its bold style and attention to detail, most famously seen in the colossal heads. Yet smaller pieces like jade masks and figurines also showcase their artistic skill.

Colossal Heads
These massive stone heads, each with unique facial features and headdress designs, may portray important rulers. Their sheer size reflects the Olmec capacity to organize and execute large-scale works.

Jade and Greenstone Art
Precious stones like jade were carved into masks, figurines, and ornaments. These items appear far from the Gulf Coast, indicating broad trade networks or strong cultural influence.

Monumental Stelae and Altars
Carved stone altars often show figures emerging from cave-like openings or holding infants. Stelae sometimes include early glyphs, hinting at the roots of Mesoamerican writing.

2.5 Religious Beliefs and Ceremonies

Olmec religion likely revolved around natural forces, ancestors, and powerful animal spirits like the jaguar. Many artworks feature a half-human, half-jaguar entity known as the were-jaguar.

The Jaguar Cult
The jaguar—an apex predator in the region—symbolized strength, fertility, and possibly a link between rulers and the divine. Some figures or rulers may have claimed descent from jaguar deities.

Sacred Ballgames
Rubber balls discovered at Olmec sites indicate a form of ballgame, possibly an early version of the ritual game later seen among the Maya and Aztecs. These games might have had spiritual significance, reflecting cosmic battles or seasonal cycles.

2.6 Trade Networks and Cultural Influence

The Olmecs traded widely, exchanging rubber, salt, cacao, and crafted goods for obsidian, jade, and other luxury materials. Their art style, religious concepts, and building methods spread across Mesoamerica.

Diffusion of Art and Iconography
Distinct Olmec motifs, such as the jaguar-human hybrid, appear in later cultures. This suggests the Olmecs played a role in shaping religious symbols that endured for centuries.

Interaction with Other Regions
Olmec traders connected the Gulf Coast to highland zones and beyond. These trade routes likely carried not just objects but also ideas and cultural practices.

2.7 Decline and Legacy

By about 400 BCE, major Olmec centers had fallen. Reasons might include environmental changes, shifting trade networks, or social upheavals. Even so, the Olmecs left a lasting impact.

Influence on Writing and Calendar

Artifacts like Tres Zapotes' Stela C suggest the Olmecs experimented with early writing or notation systems. Their innovations may have seeded the later Maya script and calendar.

Foundations for Future Civilizations

Through their organized labor, grand ceremonial spaces, and symbolic art, the Olmecs set important precedents. Later groups—Maya, Zapotecs, and eventually the Aztecs—would build upon these cultural and technological foundations.

2.8 Summary of the Olmec Epoch

The Olmecs laid essential groundwork for the complexity that defined Mesoamerica. Their masterful art, intricate religion, and extensive trade tied together vast regions. While they eventually declined, the memory of their colossal heads and influential culture would persist in the artistic and religious traditions of future civilizations.

As we move forward, Chapter 3 will discuss the Zapotecs and their capital of Monte Albán in the Oaxaca Valley. Just like the Olmecs, the Zapotecs contributed key innovations in urban planning, religion, and early writing, showing how each region built upon the achievements of those who came before.

CHAPTER 3

The Zapotecs and Monte Albán (circa 700 BCE – 800 CE)

The Zapotec civilization rose in the fertile valleys of Oaxaca, located in the southern highlands of what is now Mexico. Their story is one of determination, innovation, and a drive to create a lasting urban and cultural presence. Monte Albán, built atop a leveled mountain ridge, became their most important city and a major center in Mesoamerica. This chapter will explore how the Zapotecs formed their society, constructed enduring monuments, and established some of the earliest known writing systems in the region. We will also look at how they traded, fought wars, and interacted with neighboring peoples.

3.1 Early Zapotec Origins

Long before Monte Albán became a dominant urban center, smaller communities thrived in the valleys of Oaxaca. The region is characterized by a mix of fertile plains, rugged mountains, and microclimates that allowed for diverse agricultural practices. These early farming villages date back as far as 1500 BCE, though they were not politically unified.

Influence from Surrounding Cultures
In these early centuries, the Zapotecs may have interacted with or observed more established cultures such as the Olmecs in the Gulf Coast region. While they did not copy Olmec traditions directly, shared motifs in pottery or possibly in religious symbolism show that they were not isolated. Ideas, goods, and sometimes even rituals traveled through trade routes and migration. Over time, local leaders emerged, focusing on social organization, religious ceremonies, and the defense of their communities.

Language and Identity
The term "Zapotec" actually refers to a family of closely related languages spoken by various groups across the region. Each group had its own local identity, but over centuries, some of these communities formed alliances or exerted control over weaker neighbors. This process of consolidation laid the groundwork for the political structure that would later center at Monte Albán.

3.2 The Setting of the Oaxaca Valley

The Oaxaca Valley is a cluster of three smaller valleys: the Etla, the Tlacolula, and the Valle Grande (or Zimatlán-Ocotlán). They converge near the site of modern-day Oaxaca City. This geography offers a range of climates: higher elevations can be cooler and drier, while lower areas might receive more rainfall. Maize, beans, squash, and chili peppers became staple crops, but local variations in temperature and rainfall prompted some groups to specialize in particular foods or crafts.

Key Resources

- **Agricultural lands:** Fertile soils near rivers sustained steady farming.
- **Stone quarries:** The region provided stone for building and carving monuments.
- **Obsidian sources (though mostly outside the valley):** Important for tools, found through trade with other regions.

The varied environment helped ensure that different communities could complement each other economically, encouraging local trade well before any single capital emerged. Over time, competition for the best farmland or control of trade routes may have driven conflicts, accelerating political unification under strong leaders.

3.3 Monte Albán: The Birth of a Major City

Monte Albán arose around 500 BCE on a mountain ridge overlooking the valleys. Its founders chose a strategic location: it was high enough to survey the surrounding lands, providing a defensive advantage. Yet, the people had to level large portions of the ridge to create plazas, temples, and living quarters.

Construction and Urban Planning
The earliest phase of Monte Albán shows a central plaza surrounded by platforms on which temples and elite residences were built. Over generations, new construction phases expanded the city. Workers carved out terraces on the hillsides for farming, enabling them to feed a growing population.

Ceremonial Core

At the heart of Monte Albán lay a ceremonial precinct. Temples, palaces, and ballcourts clustered around a grand plaza. This layout indicates a strong religious-political authority, presumably led by a ruling class or priestly elite who organized large labor projects.

Danzantes (The "Dancers")

One of Monte Albán's most striking early features is a series of carved stone slabs known as *Danzantes*. These carvings show human figures in contorted poses, with facial expressions that suggest pain or trance. They may depict war captives, people in ritualistic states, or figures undergoing transformation. Some scholars argue these could also be early examples of Zapotec writing mixed with symbolic images.

3.4 Society, Government, and Religion

As Monte Albán flourished, the Zapotecs developed a complex social structure. A ruling elite, likely including both secular and religious authorities, managed resources, commanded warriors, and conducted grand rituals. The city's architecture and art reflect the power of these leaders, who claimed divine or semi-divine status to legitimize their rule.

Leadership and Hierarchy
Nobles lived in palatial homes near the ceremonial core, while commoners occupied simpler dwellings on the terraces and surrounding farmland. Artisans specialized in pottery, weaving, or stone carving, producing items that elites used in religious ceremonies or traded with other regions.

Religion and Ritual
Religion played a central role in unifying the people. Temples served as hubs for offerings, ancestor veneration, and possibly astronomical observations. Priests performed rituals that might include bloodletting or other forms of sacrifice, seeking to maintain cosmic balance and ensure agricultural fertility. The city's alignment may also reflect sacred cosmological ideas: certain buildings appear oriented to solar or stellar events.

Funerary Customs
Elaborate tombs discovered beneath Monte Albán's structures suggest a belief in the afterlife or ancestral power. These tombs, often adorned with painted murals, contained offerings of pottery, jewelry, and sometimes precious stones. Rulers and elites were likely interred with objects symbolizing status, reflecting their importance even after death.

3.5 The Zapotec Writing System

Among the notable accomplishments at Monte Albán is the development of an early writing system. The Zapotec script, although not fully deciphered, shows that they used glyphs or symbols to record genealogies, conquests, and religious information.

Origins and Influence
Some scholars believe the Zapotec system was influenced by earlier Olmec symbols, while others propose it emerged independently due to the needs of an increasingly complex society. Regardless, it stands as one of the earliest forms of writing in Mesoamerica, paralleling or even predating the earliest Maya writing.

Use in Political and Ritual Contexts
Writing was likely reserved for critical matters: royal proclamations, historical events, or sacred knowledge. Stone stelae and building inscriptions show short texts, often accompanied by images of rulers or deities. This blend of pictorial art and written symbols helped record political victories or alliances.

3.6 Daily Life and Economy

While the grandeur of Monte Albán's temples and tombs reveals the sophistication of elite life, day-to-day routines for most Zapotecs revolved around agriculture, craft production, and family obligations.

Farming Communities
Most people lived outside the ceremonial center in terraced fields or small villages. They produced maize, beans, squash, and other crops central to the Mesoamerican diet. Seasonal labor patterns might involve extended families working communal plots, with certain times of the year set aside for large construction or ritual events in the city.

Market Exchanges
Though not as extensive as later Aztec markets, the Zapotecs likely organized periodic markets where farmers and artisans traded food, pottery, textiles, and other goods. These markets strengthened bonds between city dwellers and rural producers.

Craft Specialization
Skilled artisans made cotton textiles, polished stone beads, and high-quality pottery decorated with geometric or religious motifs. Some artisans resided in Monte Albán or nearby centers, possibly supplying the elite class with luxury items. Others traveled to smaller communities, trading or teaching local craftspeople.

3.7 Relations with Neighboring Cultures

The Zapotecs did not exist in isolation. Monte Albán's strategic location allowed them to influence the valleys around them, and even beyond. Artifacts and inscriptions hint at both trade and warfare with other cultures.

Trade Routes
Goods such as obsidian from distant volcanic regions, tropical bird feathers, and seashells from the coasts flowed through the Oaxaca Valley. In return, Zapotec pottery, textiles, and possibly specialized agricultural products moved outward. This commerce linked the Zapotec heartland to the broader Mesoamerican world.

Military Campaigns

Carvings at Monte Albán depict bound captives, city glyphs that may represent conquered towns, and scenes that suggest warfare. By subduing neighboring polities, Zapotec rulers could control trade routes or vital farmland. These displays reinforced the power and prestige of Monte Albán's elite.

Diplomatic Marriages

Marriage alliances between ruling families might have been another avenue for maintaining peace or exerting influence. By marrying into lineages from other cities, the Zapotec elite could create personal and political bonds that limited open conflict and promoted cooperation.

3.8 Shifts and Decline

Around 200 CE, Monte Albán reached its peak in population and cultural influence. The city's core expanded, and new building projects continued. Over time, however, changes in trade routes and political rivalries emerged, both within the valley and beyond. By about 600 CE, there were signs of decline.

Possible Causes

- **Economic Competition:** Other centers in Mesoamerica, including Teotihuacan and later the Maya polities, might have overshadowed Monte Albán in trade and political influence.
- **Internal Strife:** Rival factions within the Zapotec territory may have weakened central authority.
- **Environmental Stress:** Deforestation, soil depletion, or extended droughts could have impacted the agricultural base.

By around 800 CE, Monte Albán no longer served as the supreme power in the region. People did not abandon it entirely, but it lost the status of a bustling capital. Later Mixtec influences became strong in parts of Oaxaca, further diminishing the city's Zapotec dominance.

3.9 Legacy of the Zapotecs

Though Monte Albán's era of major building and expansion ended, the Zapotec civilization did not vanish. They persisted in the region, adapting to new political realities. Their language and cultural traditions survived into the colonial period and still exist today among modern Zapotec communities.

Contributions to Mesoamerican Civilization

- **Urban Engineering:** Building a city atop a mountain plateau showed tremendous planning.
- **Writing System:** Their script stands as one of the earliest in Mesoamerica, proving their scholarly capabilities.
- **Artistic Heritage:** Pottery, carved stones, and tomb murals reflect a deep cultural identity that influenced later groups.

Understanding the Zapotecs helps us appreciate the diversity of pre-Hispanic Mexico. Their unique blend of innovation and tradition contributed to the mosaic of Mesoamerican societies. Monte Albán, with its spectacular vistas and enduring ruins, remains a key testament to their achievements.

By exploring the Zapotec rise and the prominence of Monte Albán, we see how regional power centers could develop sophisticated cultures while engaging in both cooperation and conflict with their neighbors. In the next chapter, we will shift our focus to one of the largest and most influential cities in the ancient Americas: Teotihuacan. Known to later peoples as the "City of the Gods," Teotihuacan's scale and architectural grandeur would shape the course of Mesoamerican history for centuries.

CHAPTER 4

Teotihuacan – The City of the Gods (circa 100 BCE – 650 CE)

As Monte Albán thrived in the Oaxaca Valley, another monumental city rose in the Basin of Mexico. Teotihuacan would become one of the most populous and influential urban centers of the ancient world. Its grand pyramids, orderly streets, and far-reaching trade networks left a lasting imprint on Mesoamerica. Even the Aztecs, arriving centuries later, revered it as a sacred place of origins. This chapter examines Teotihuacan's founding, its urban planning, its social life, and the mysteries surrounding its decline.

4.1 Environmental and Geographical Background

Teotihuacan stands in a highland basin northeast of modern-day Mexico City. This area, at roughly 2,200 meters (7,200 feet) above sea level, has a temperate climate with distinct dry and rainy seasons. Nearby sources of obsidian, fertile soils for agriculture, and crucial trade routes passing through the region all favored urban development.

The Basin of Mexico
A ring of volcanic mountains encloses the basin, creating a resource-rich environment. Lakes once covered much of the valley floor, providing fish, waterfowl, and aquatic plants. Although the lakes have mostly disappeared today, in ancient times they supported large populations.

Choice of Location
Teotihuacan's founders selected a spot near the San Juan River. They likely valued the river for irrigation and transportation. Over decades, the city expanded across the floodplain, developing into a planned metropolis that would house tens of thousands of people.

4.2 Urban Planning and Architecture

Teotihuacan is remarkable for its grid-like urban design, which was rare in ancient times. Major roads, such as the "Avenue of the Dead," structured the city's layout. This main avenue stretches for several kilometers and aligns with important ceremonial complexes.

Central Precinct

Near the middle of the avenue stand key structures: the Pyramid of the Sun, the Pyramid of the Moon, and the Ciudadela (Citadel), which encloses the Temple of the Feathered Serpent. Residential compounds spread out around these major monuments. Many residences included apartment-like complexes with courtyards, decorated walls, and drainage systems.

Building Materials and Techniques

Teotihuacan builders used stone, adobe, and rubble fill. Facades were often decorated with plaster and bright paints, especially shades of red. Murals featuring gods, animals, and symbolic motifs adorned household and public spaces, reflecting a shared religious and cultural identity.

Monumental Scale

At its peak, Teotihuacan's urban area covered roughly 20 square kilometers (about 8 square miles). This scale required meticulous planning, a strong governing authority, and the labor of many workers. Large public construction projects likely took place in stages over generations, suggesting consistent political stability for a significant period.

4.3 The Pyramids: Sun and Moon

Two of Teotihuacan's iconic structures are the Pyramid of the Sun and the Pyramid of the Moon, both situated along the Avenue of the Dead.

Pyramid of the Sun

Rising over 60 meters (200 feet), the Pyramid of the Sun is among the largest structures of its kind in Mesoamerica. A monumental staircase leads to the summit, which may have held a small temple. Some tunnels or caves lie beneath the pyramid's foundation, possibly used for rituals linked to underworld beliefs.

Pyramid of the Moon

Slightly smaller than its neighbor but still imposing, the Pyramid of the Moon anchors the northern end of the avenue. It faces a plaza where public ceremonies and gatherings might have taken place. Offerings found under its base include obsidian blades, animal bones, and figurines, suggesting ritual significance.

Ceremonial Focus

Both pyramids likely served as focal points for religious festivities. Priests or rulers conducted rites from their summits, visible to large crowds gathered below. The architectural alignment might also connect to astronomical events, such as equinoxes or solstices, reflecting the city's cosmological worldview.

4.4 Teotihuacan's Social Structure and Daily Life

Despite its monumental core, most residents of Teotihuacan lived in apartment compounds. Archaeological excavations reveal that people from various social ranks coexisted: nobles, artisans, traders, and common laborers. Some compounds show wealthier homes with frescoes and imported goods, while others appear more modest.

Multi-Ethnic Neighborhoods

Evidence points to foreign communities within the city, including people from the Gulf Coast, Oaxaca, and the Maya region. These enclaves likely formed through migration and long-distance trade relationships. Each group retained aspects of its cultural traditions, contributing to the city's diversity.

Craft Production

Teotihuacan was a major manufacturing hub. Obsidian workshops produced tools, blades, and ritual objects. Skilled artisans painted murals, carved stone statues, and made pottery. Elite-sponsored craft specialists might have lived in specific districts, while others sold their work in local markets.

Gender Roles and Family

Households might include extended families working cooperatively. Women likely engaged in weaving and food preparation; men might handle building tasks, farming, or specialized crafts. Religious activities could involve both genders, although high-ranking priests were often male.

4.5 Religion and Iconography

Teotihuacan's religion remains partially mysterious, as no fully deciphered written texts exist. However, the city's art and architecture offer clues about its pantheon and ritual practices.

Major Deities
Murals and sculptures feature deities like the "Great Goddess," a figure often depicted with water or vegetation symbols, and the Feathered Serpent, associated with fertility and political power. The Storm God, similar to the later Aztec Tlaloc, appears in temple murals as well.

Temple of the Feathered Serpent (in the Ciudadela)
Elaborate carvings of serpents with feathers, combined with masks or shells, decorate the temple's facade. Burials beneath the pyramid contain numerous sacrificial victims. These rites may have been performed to sanctify the construction or honor important events in the city's history.

Mural Art
Teotihuacan's murals frequently depict processions, mythical creatures, and symbols of water and fertility. Colors like red, yellow, and green dominate, reflecting an emphasis on life-sustaining forces. Priests, rulers, or supernatural beings wearing elaborate headdresses appear in many scenes, underscoring the close relationship between religion and governance.

4.6 Trade Networks and External Influence

Part of Teotihuacan's power came from its vast trade connections. Obsidian from nearby quarries was a major export, prized by other Mesoamerican cultures for its sharp edges. Goods like pottery, textiles, and possibly agricultural products were also traded.

Long-Distance Contacts
Artifacts from Teotihuacan appear in places as far away as the Maya lowlands, suggesting active exchange of goods and ideas. In sites like Tikal (in present-day Guatemala), archaeologists have found objects in the "Teotihuacan style" and references to possible diplomatic alliances or conquests.

Cultural Exchange
Teotihuacan's influence on other regions is evident in architectural imitations, pottery styles, and the spread of particular art motifs. Rulers of distant cities might adopt Teotihuacan fashion or building layouts to associate themselves with the prestige and success of this giant metropolis.

Political Control or Symbolic Prestige?
Some scholars debate whether Teotihuacan engaged in direct military conquest or mainly used economic and cultural sway. The discovery of weapons and warrior imagery suggests that Teotihuacan elites did not shy away from force. However, the city's widespread presence could also stem from prestige: neighboring cultures may have voluntarily aligned themselves with Teotihuacan's success, seeking trade advantages and status.

4.7 The Decline of Teotihuacan

By around 550–600 CE, Teotihuacan began to face challenges. Archaeological evidence points to signs of internal unrest, including burned elite compounds near the city's core. Whether caused by peasant revolts, factional struggles among elites, or external invasions remains a subject of debate.

Environmental Strains
Population growth may have strained local resources. Soil depletion, deforestation, or shifts in climate could have impacted agricultural yields, leading to discontent among the lower classes.

Power Shifts
As Teotihuacan's influence waned, other cities in Mesoamerica rose. The Maya region, for instance, saw the emergence of powerful dynasties controlling key trade routes. If Teotihuacan's trade monopolies broke down, the city would lose economic strength, making it harder to maintain large construction projects or a standing army.

Collapse and Aftermath
By 650–700 CE, Teotihuacan's population had significantly declined. While pockets of people likely remained in the area, the monumental heart no longer functioned as a thriving capital. Later civilizations, including the Toltecs and Aztecs, recognized the ruins as a sacred place, weaving them into their own mythologies.

4.8 Legacy of Teotihuacan

Though abandoned as a major city, Teotihuacan continued to influence Mesoamerican societies. The memory of its vast pyramids, mysterious rituals, and powerful gods resonated for centuries. The Aztecs, upon seeing the site, believed it was built by giants or gods. They named it "Teotihuacan," roughly meaning "the place where the gods were born."

Artistic and Religious Influence

- **Architecture:** Later cities replicated Teotihuacan's grand plazas and stepped pyramids.
- **Iconography:** Feathered Serpent imagery, storm god depictions, and ceremonial symbolism influenced subsequent cultures like the Toltecs and Mexica (Aztecs).
- **Urban Planning:** The concept of a grid-aligned city with central avenues shaped Mesoamerican ideas about what a sacred or imperial capital should look like.

Modern Significance

Today, Teotihuacan is a major archaeological site and a UNESCO World Heritage spot. Millions of visitors climb the Pyramid of the Sun to marvel at the scale of this ancient metropolis. Ongoing research uncovers new details each year, revealing more about the city's daily life and spiritual beliefs.

Teotihuacan remains a testament to human creativity and organization. By studying its ruins, we learn about the possibilities and challenges of managing large populations, orchestrating monumental building projects, and forging widespread cultural influence.

In the next chapters, we will see how new powers rose after Teotihuacan's decline, including the Toltecs in central Mexico, the Mixtecs in Oaxaca, and eventually the Aztecs. Each inherited parts of Teotihuacan's cultural DNA, while also forging their own paths in an ever-changing mosaic of alliances, rivalries, and remarkable achievements.

CHAPTER 5

The Classic Maya (circa 250 CE – 900 CE)

The Classic Maya period was a remarkable time in Mesoamerican history. During these centuries, the Maya built thriving city-states across parts of present-day Mexico, Guatemala, Belize, Honduras, and El Salvador. They developed one of the most sophisticated writing systems in the Americas, refined complex calendars, and created monumental architecture that still amazes people today. These achievements did not happen overnight. The Maya had deep roots going back to earlier Preclassic and Formative phases, but it was in the Classic period that their civilization reached its greatest cultural, political, and artistic heights.

Below, we will explore the rise of key Maya city-states, the social and political structures that held them together, the beliefs that guided their spiritual world, the art and architecture that showcased their creativity, and the events that led to the "collapse" of many Classic centers. We will see that the story of the Classic Maya is complex. It involves alliances, wars, religious devotion, intellectual breakthroughs, and daily life for ordinary farmers and craftworkers. Their legacy would live on long after many of their great cities were abandoned.

5.1 Geographic and Environmental Diversity

Maya cities did not sit in one uniform landscape. Instead, the Maya world was spread across varied environments, from the dense tropical rainforests of the Petén region in northern Guatemala to the mountainous highlands of Chiapas and Guatemala, and eastward to the low-lying coastal plains of the Yucatán Peninsula. Each zone offered distinct resources and challenges:

- **Rainforest lowlands:** Heavy rainfall, thick forests, and sometimes nutrient-poor soils. Cities like Tikal, Calakmul, and Yaxchilán emerged here.
- **Highlands:** Cooler temperatures, volcanic soil, and valuable stones like obsidian and jade. Kaminaljuyú near modern Guatemala City was once an important highland center.
- **Northern plains of the Yucatán Peninsula:** More arid region with less rainfall, requiring unique water management systems, as seen in sites like Uxmal or Chichén Itzá (though the latter flourished more in the Postclassic).

This environmental diversity shaped different farming methods, city layouts, and even social organization. For instance, water management was crucial in the drier regions, while in the rainforest, large-scale slash-and-burn agriculture and raised fields were used to maximize food production. Across these areas, however, the Maya shared many cultural traits—language families, religious practices, and a mutual reverence for maize as the staple crop and spiritual symbol of life.

5.2 Political Landscape: Independent but Connected City-States

Classic Maya civilization was never a single empire under one ruler. Instead, it consisted of many city-states, each with its own royal dynasty. These polities formed webs of alliances and rivalries, competing for resources, trade routes, and tribute from smaller towns. Sometimes they cooperated in ceremonial events or intermarried royal families to seal peace treaties, but they could also engage in warfare to capture prisoners, expand influence, or resolve dynastic disputes.

Examples of Major Centers

- **Tikal:** Located in the Petén Basin, it emerged as a major power early in the Classic period, controlling trade routes and subjugating nearby communities at times.
- **Calakmul:** A rival to Tikal, based in what is now the Mexican state of Campeche. The city often vied with Tikal for regional dominance.
- **Palenque:** Situated in the Chiapas region of Mexico, Palenque became known for its exquisite architecture and the rule of famed kings like K'inich Janaab' Pakal.
- **Copán:** Located in modern Honduras, Copán was a key intellectual and artistic center. Its stelae show detailed inscriptions of royal lineages.
- **Yaxchilán:** Positioned along the Usumacinta River, known for intricately carved lintels depicting royal rituals.

While these major centers shaped the political balance, smaller sites also played roles, sometimes acting as client states or forming defensive alliances. Regular diplomacy involved marriage alliances that joined dynasties together. At times, a large kingdom might have "vassal" cities that paid tribute or followed their lead in wars. However, no single capital ever unified all the Maya under one banner.

5.3 Maya Kingship and Dynasties

At the heart of each city-state stood the *Ajaw* (often translated as "lord" or "king"). Maya rulers claimed a divine or semi-divine status, linking themselves to the gods through rituals and blood ties. They were central figures in both the religious and political spheres, responsible for ensuring the prosperity of their people by communing with supernatural forces.

Royal Functions

- **Leading rituals:** These ranged from bloodletting (using stingray spines or obsidian blades) to large public ceremonies aimed at appeasing deities.
- **Overseeing warfare:** Successful military campaigns boosted a king's prestige. Captives might be sacrificed in important rituals, particularly to honor the city's patron gods.
- **Building monuments:** Rulers commissioned pyramids, temples, and stelae to display their genealogies and achievements.
- **Maintaining cosmic order:** The Maya believed that kings, through correct performance of rituals and alignment with the calendar, kept the universe balanced and fertile.

Royal Succession
Dynastic lines were carefully recorded in stone carvings, especially on stelae or temple tablets. A successor was often a son of the previous king, though exceptions occurred. Queens sometimes ruled in their own right if circumstances demanded. Each accession to the throne was marked by elaborate ceremonies, often including symbolic acts of rebirth tying the new ruler to cosmic events.

5.4 Social Hierarchy and Daily Life

Maya society was stratified, but it also relied on the constant labor of commoners who made up the majority of the population. Studying how ordinary people lived helps us understand the broader achievements of the civilization.

Nobles and Priests
The upper classes included nobles who held administrative or ceremonial roles, often related to the royal court. Priests specialized in calendar calculations, divination, and performing sacred rituals. Scribes and artists also ranked high in status, given the importance of recording history and crafting royal iconography.

Commoners

Farmers, laborers, and craftworkers formed the backbone of Maya society. They produced the food and materials that sustained cities. Many lived in thatched homes built on low platforms near agricultural fields. Extended families might share compounds, working together on tasks like planting maize, beans, and squash, or tending to small livestock like turkeys and dogs.

Trade and Craft Production

Skilled artisans created pottery, wove textiles, and fashioned stone tools or obsidian blades. Traders traveled by canoe along rivers and coastal routes or by foot through jungle paths. Goods like salt, cacao beans (used both as currency and for making chocolate drinks), jade, quetzal feathers, and fine ceramics moved between regions. Markets in major cities facilitated exchange, while long-distance trade networks tied the Maya world together.

5.5 Maya Writing and Knowledge Systems

One of the defining features of the Maya was their advanced writing system, known as Maya hieroglyphs. This script combined pictorial symbols (representing objects or concepts) with phonetic elements (representing sounds). It took scholars centuries to decode, but modern epigraphers have made tremendous progress, revealing an intricate record of history, mythology, and daily events.

Hieroglyphic Texts

- **Stelae and Altars:** Tall stone monuments set in ceremonial plazas often carried lengthy inscriptions about a ruler's lineage, key victories, or important calendar dates.
- **Temple Inscriptions:** Inside palaces and temples, carved panels recounted the exploits of kings and queens, weaving mythic origins into real historical events.
- **Codices:** The Maya produced folded bark-paper books, called codices, filled with astronomical data, religious rituals, and genealogical records. Most were destroyed during the Spanish Conquest, but a few, such as the Dresden Codex, survived.

Astronomy and Calendar

The Maya were expert sky-watchers. They tracked celestial bodies to develop precise calendars, which they used for planning crop cycles, scheduling rituals, and recording historical events. Two important cycles included:

1. **Tzolk'in:** A 260-day ritual calendar.
2. **Haab':** A 365-day solar calendar, similar to a year.

Together, they formed a larger cyclical system known as the Calendar Round, repeating every 52 years. The Maya also employed the **Long Count** calendar for recording long spans of time from a mythic starting point. Observatories, like those at Caracol (Belize) or some structures in Chichén Itzá (though mainly Postclassic), helped priests track movements of Venus, the sun, and the moon with impressive accuracy.

5.6 Religion, Cosmology, and Deities

Maya religion was deeply complex, with a rich pantheon of gods governing various natural and cosmic forces. Religious ceremonies ensured the continued harmony between gods, humans, and the environment. Sacrifice, often involving the shedding of royal blood, was seen as a potent offering that sustained the divine energies.

Major Deities

- **Itzamna:** Often regarded as a creator deity, associated with writing and wisdom.
- **Chac:** The rain god, especially critical in the humid lowlands but venerated throughout the Maya region due to the dependence on rainfall for crops.
- **K'awiil (God K):** A deity linked to royal power, often portrayed with a serpent foot or a lightning axe.
- **Ix Chel:** A goddess linked to the moon, childbirth, and healing.

Sacred Geography

Caves, cenotes (sinkholes), and mountaintops held special significance as entrances to the underworld or realms of the gods. Offerings of pottery, jade, or even human sacrifices were placed in these locations to communicate with deities. The city layout often mirrored cosmic beliefs, with temples serving as man-made "mountains" bridging heaven and earth.

Ritual Practices

- **Bloodletting:** A crucial ceremony in which rulers or priests would pierce their tongues or other body parts, offering blood on paper or cloth burned as incense.
- **Human Sacrifice:** Although less prevalent than in some later cultures, it was still performed, especially for dedicating new buildings or celebrating major military victories.
- **Communal Festivals:** People of all classes participated in cyclical feasts that aligned with calendar events or agricultural milestones.

5.7 Architecture and Urban Design

Maya cities featured grand plazas surrounded by temple-pyramids, palaces, ballcourts, and administrative buildings. Each architectural element served religious, political, or social purposes.

Temple-Pyramids
These stepped structures rose above the surrounding jungle canopy. Typically, a small sanctuary crowned the top, where priests or rulers performed rituals. Famous examples include Tikal's Temple I and Temple II, which towered over the main plaza.

Palaces
Royal courts and noble residences often consisted of multi-room complexes with courtyards. In Palenque, for example, the royal palace featured a distinctive four-story tower. Walls of these complexes sometimes held elaborate stucco carvings painted in bright reds, blues, and yellows.

Ballcourts
The Mesoamerican ballgame had both recreational and ritual significance. Maya ballcourts varied in size but shared a basic design: two sloping walls flanking a playing alley. Games might re-enact mythic battles between gods of life and death. In some ceremonies, losing captives were sacrificed.

Stelae and Altars
Plazas were often adorned with stelae, each representing a moment in the city's dynastic history. Circular or rectangular altars might sit before the stelae, possibly used for offerings or commemorations of specific events.

5.8 Warfare, Diplomacy, and Shifting Alliances

Classic Maya history was marked by both cultural achievements and bouts of intense warfare. Inscriptions reveal conflicts over trade routes, political rivalries, and dynastic disputes. Military campaigns often aimed to capture high-status individuals from enemy cities rather than annex large territories as in modern wars.

Captive-Taking and Ritual
Captives, especially noble or royal relatives of rival kings, had symbolic importance. Their capture demonstrated dominance. They could be ransomed, forced to serve the victor's city, or sacrificed to appease gods. This practice enhanced the prestige of successful warriors and rulers.

Key Rivalry: Tikal vs. Calakmul
These two major powers repeatedly vied for hegemony in the central lowlands. Each city gathered smaller allies around it. At times, Tikal fell under the influence of Teotihuacan (in central Mexico), while Calakmul forged alliances with other powerful states. Texts record battles, victories, defeats, and periods of uneasy peace.

Diplomatic Marriages

Royal families often arranged marriages between kingdoms to solidify alliances. A princess from one city might become the queen of another, linking dynasties and reducing the likelihood of conflict. But alliances were fragile and could break down if a new ruler sought more aggressive expansion.

5.9 Economic Foundations and Trade Networks

Beneath the splendor of kings and temples lay an economic system that supported Maya civilization. Farming was the core, but specialized crafts and long-distance trade also played vital roles.

Agricultural Methods

- **Milpa (slash-and-burn):** Farmers cleared forests, burned vegetation for nutrients, then planted maize, beans, and squash. After several harvests, fields were left fallow to regenerate.
- **Terracing and Raised Fields:** In regions with heavy rainfall or uneven terrain, terraces prevented erosion, and raised fields improved drainage.
- **Chinampas (floating gardens):** Less common than with the later Aztecs, but some Maya groups used similar methods where feasible.

Trade Goods

- **Obsidian:** Razor-sharp volcanic glass used for tools and weapons; circulated widely across the Maya region.
- **Jade and Exotic Stones:** Used for elite jewelry and ceremonial objects, symbolizing power.
- **Cacao:** Valued for making chocolate drinks, also used as a form of currency in some areas.
- **Salt:** Essential for dietary needs and food preservation; coastal salt pans were significant.
- **Textiles:** Cotton cloth, dyed or embroidered, served as markers of status.

Markets within large cities drew people from surrounding countryside. The overlapping trade routes tied the Maya lowlands and highlands together, and also connected the Maya to distant regions such as central Mexico or the Gulf Coast. Traders not only exchanged goods but also brought information, ideas, and possibly religious practices.

5.10 Intellectual and Artistic Achievements

The Maya did not just build large cities; they filled them with refined artistry and intellectual work. This included painting, sculpture, pottery, and advanced knowledge of mathematics and astronomy.

Mathematics
The Maya used a vigesimal (base-20) numeric system, which included the concept of zero—one of the earliest known uses of zero in the world. This allowed them to make complex calendar calculations and keep records of dates spanning hundreds or even thousands of years.

Murals and Painted Ceramics
Maya murals found at sites like Bonampak depict warfare, courtly life, and ritual dances in vivid colors. Painted ceramics, often used as grave goods, feature mythic scenes, daily activities, or noble feasts. These vessels also carried hieroglyphic texts naming the owner or the pot's intended contents.

Stucco and Stone Carvings
Walls, lintels, and facades were adorned with stucco reliefs showing gods, rulers, or mythical creatures. Stone lintels at Yaxchilán famously depict queens performing bloodletting rituals or presenting captives to victorious kings. The artistry shows a high level of skill in both carving and storytelling.

5.11 The Collapse of Classic Maya Cities

Around the 8th and 9th centuries CE, many southern lowland cities—including Tikal, Palenque, and Copán—experienced a sharp decline. Populations dwindled, monumental building ceased, and stelae were no longer dedicated. Scholars debate the factors behind this "collapse," which was not uniform across all Maya regions.

Possible Contributing Factors

1. **Environmental Stress:** Extended droughts, deforestation, and soil depletion may have crippled agriculture. Evidence from lake sediments shows periods of reduced rainfall.

2. **Warfare and Political Instability:** As rivalries intensified, cities may have exhausted their resources in ongoing conflicts. Wars disrupted trade routes and made farmland unsafe.
3. **Social Unrest:** Commoners could have lost faith in rulers who failed to secure enough food or quell warfare, leading to revolts or mass migrations.
4. **Disease:** Epidemics may have swept through, although evidence is less direct.

It is important to note that while the southern lowlands saw the most severe depopulation, some cities in the northern Yucatán, like those around the Puuc hills region (e.g., Uxmal), continued to flourish into the Postclassic. The idea of a sudden, total "collapse" is somewhat misleading. Maya civilization did not vanish overnight; it transformed as power centers shifted northward.

5.12 Legacy of the Classic Maya

The Classic Maya left behind magnificent ruins that still draw explorers and tourists. Their achievements in writing, astronomy, and art were extraordinary. Many Maya people today maintain elements of their ancestors' culture, including language, traditional practices, and agricultural methods. The knowledge we have gleaned from deciphered hieroglyphs has given us unique insights into the daily concerns, wars, alliances, and spiritual beliefs of an ancient civilization.

Continued Cultural Resilience

Maya communities did not disappear. In the centuries after the Classic "collapse," new centers emerged, especially in the northern Yucatán, giving rise to major Postclassic cities like Chichén Itzá and Mayapán. Even under Spanish colonial rule, Maya groups preserved some traditions, resisting full assimilation.

Modern Importance

Archaeological excavations and decipherment efforts are ongoing, revealing fresh data each year. The modern Maya, living in the same geographic areas, often collaborate with researchers, sharing knowledge and perspectives. Together, they bring the rich heritage of the Classic Maya period into clearer focus for the world.

After traversing the Classic Maya world—its majestic cities, scholarly pursuits, and enduring legacies—we now turn to another major power in Mesoamerica: the Toltecs. In **Chapter 6**, we will explore how the Toltecs rose to prominence in central Mexico after the decline of Teotihuacan, weaving myths and historical events that eventually influenced the Aztecs.

CHAPTER 6

The Toltecs and Tula (circa 900 CE – 1150 CE)

After the decline of Teotihuacan around the 7th and 8th centuries CE, central Mexico entered a period of political fragmentation. Various groups vied for influence, forging alliances and sometimes engaging in conflict. Out of this environment, the Toltecs emerged as a dominant force. Their capital city, Tula (also known as Tollan), became a center of political power, commerce, and cultural activity. Later Aztec legends would remember the Toltecs as refined master builders and teachers of noble arts, creating a mix of myth and fact that still fascinates historians today.

In this chapter, we will discuss who the Toltecs were, how Tula grew into a key metropolis, what cultural innovations they introduced, and how their influence spread. We will also see how the Toltec legacy, whether real or romanticized, left a deep mark on the later Aztec worldview.

6.1 The Postclassic Context

The Postclassic period (roughly 900 CE to 1521 CE) saw significant changes in Mesoamerica. Large-scale states of the Classic era, such as those led by Teotihuacan in central Mexico or by powerful Maya kingdoms in the southern lowlands, had declined or transformed. In central Mexico, many smaller city-states rose and fell until one group or coalition gained the upper hand.

Rise of New Powers

- Toltecs in the north-central highlands
- Postclassic Maya in the Yucatán (Chichén Itzá, Mayapán)
- Mixtec dominance in parts of Oaxaca

Trade routes shifted, carrying metals like copper from West Mexico and turquoise from the north. Military technology evolved, with the wider use of bows and arrows, making warfare more dynamic than in the Classic period. The Toltecs capitalized on these shifting trade connections, building a network that helped Tula become a commercial hub.

6.2 Who Were the Toltecs?

The exact origins of the Toltecs remain somewhat shrouded in legend and patchy archaeology. Some scholars link them to the earlier inhabitants of Teotihuacan or to northern nomadic groups that gradually moved south. The name "Toltec" in Nahuatl can mean "skilled artisan," which later Aztecs used as a broad label for anyone of particularly refined skill. The term eventually came to mean both a people and a cultural ideal.

Ethnic and Linguistic Background
Many researchers believe the Toltecs spoke a form of Nahuatl or a closely related language. The Aztecs, who also spoke Nahuatl, considered the Toltecs their cultural ancestors. Aztec chronicles merge real Toltec history with myths, crediting the Toltecs for all sorts of advancements in art, architecture, and religion. It can be tricky to separate fact from legend.

Migration Traditions
Aztec stories include accounts of different groups migrating into the Basin of Mexico. Some of these tales might preserve memories of actual population shifts that occurred in the wake of Teotihuacan's fall. Tula stands out in these stories as an important city founded or revived by Toltec lineages who rose to prominence around the 10th century CE.

6.3 The City of Tula (Tollan)

Located in present-day Hidalgo, Tula was strategically positioned near trade routes linking the northern frontiers (rich in mineral resources) and the heart of central Mexico. The city itself had two main ceremonial areas, marked by pyramids, ballcourts, and plazas. Over time, Tula grew into a sprawling urban center with residential zones, workshops, and fortifications.

Key Architectural Features

- **Pyramid B:** Often called the Temple of Tlahuizcalpantecuhtli (the so-called "Temple of the Morning Star"), it is topped by massive warrior columns known as the Atlantean figures.

- **Atlantean Columns:** Carved stone pillars depicting armed warriors with distinct headdresses and butterfly pectorals. They once supported the temple roof.
- **Palaces and Ballcourts:** Tula contained at least two ballcourts and evidence of administrative buildings near the pyramids.
- **Residential Districts:** Clay figurines, spindle whorls, and obsidian tools hint at daily crafts. Many inhabitants likely farmed on terraces nearby or traded goods.

Population and Defense

Archaeologists estimate Tula may have housed tens of thousands of people at its peak, with farmland surrounding the central districts. Walls or ramparts suggest concerns about external threats or rival polities.

6.4 Toltec Religion and Mythology

Toltec religion is not as well documented as that of the Aztecs or Classic Maya, but some iconography and later Aztec narratives shed light on their major deities and beliefs. The worship of Quetzalcoatl (the Feathered Serpent) played a central role in many tales about Tula.

Quetzalcoatl Myths

Aztec sources describe a legendary Toltec priest-king named Topiltzin Quetzalcoatl, who encouraged peaceful worship and discouraged human sacrifice. In these stories, he was tricked by rivals and driven from Tula, fleeing east to the Gulf Coast. These legends blend real historical persons, such as certain Toltec rulers, with the symbolism of Quetzalcoatl as a deity of learning, wind, and fertility.

Tlahuizcalpantecuhtli (Morning Star)

Some inscriptions or artwork refer to Tlahuizcalpantecuhtli, an aspect of Quetzalcoatl linked with the planet Venus. The warrior pillars on Pyramid B at Tula carry motifs that might connect them to this star deity.

Religious Practices

Although the Aztecs depicted the Toltecs as more enlightened, there is archaeological evidence for human sacrifice at Tula, including burnt remains and dedicated offering pits. The ballgame also had ritual significance, and altars or braziers used in ceremonies suggest typical Mesoamerican religious activities, though the precise rituals remain unclear.

6.5 Toltec Art and Architecture

Toltec art is often recognized for its strong, militaristic themes. Many carvings and sculptures emphasize warriors, jaguars, eagles, and symbols of sacrifice. This contrasts with the more cosmic or natural motifs frequently seen in Classic Maya art.

Atlantean Figures
These towering basalt columns represent warriors with short kilts, butterfly pectorals, and distinctive headdresses. They likely carried spears or atlatls in their arms, now broken away. The style is somewhat geometric and bold, reflecting an emphasis on power and order.

Reliefs and Sculptures
Stone reliefs at Tula depict eagles consuming hearts, a motif later adopted by the Aztecs. Feline imagery (especially jaguars) also appears. These carvings suggest the importance of military might, sacrificial offerings, and the connection of warriors to the spiritual realm.

Pottery and Crafts
Toltec ceramics included plumbate ware (a shiny, hard pottery type) and other vessels traded widely. Figurines, some representing deities and others depicting everyday life, appear in household contexts. Trade in obsidian tools, turquoise, and shell goods helped maintain Tula's economy and extended its cultural reach.

6.6 Military Expansion and Influence

By combining trade relationships with strategic military campaigns, the Toltecs grew their sphere of influence. Some researchers believe Tula controlled a network of smaller sites, possibly collecting tribute in resources or labor. Evidence of Toltec-style artifacts appears in areas like the Gulf Coast and parts of the Yucatán, suggesting broad connections.

Relations with Other Regions

- **Chichén Itzá:** Some similarities in art and architecture led early scholars to propose that Toltecs invaded the northern Maya lowlands, influencing Chichén Itzá. The exact nature of this "Toltec-Maya" connection is debated, but the shared imagery of feathered serpents and warrior columns is striking.
- **Western and Northern Mexico:** Items such as copper bells and turquoise arrived from the northwest, passing through Toltec-controlled trade routes. Tula's strategic location might have allowed it to mediate the movement of valuable goods.
- **Central Mexico Rivalries:** Not all central Mexican groups accepted Toltec dominance. There may have been ongoing conflicts with other city-states, though the details are sparse.

Military Technology
Toltec warriors used the **atlatl** (spear-thrower), bows, arrows, and obsidian-bladed clubs. Elite warriors might also have worn elaborate feathered costumes or carried symbolic regalia linked to deities like Tezcatlipoca or Quetzalcoatl.

6.7 Society and Daily Life in Tula

Although the Toltecs are famed for their warrior culture, Tula's inhabitants included various social classes and occupations. Archaeological evidence reveals aspects of daily life beyond the ceremonial centers.

Social Stratification

- **Ruling Elite:** Possibly led by a single king or a small council of nobles who controlled trade, tribute collection, and religious ceremonies.

- **Priests and Military Officers:** Held significant status. Priests managed ritual calendars and temple activities, while officers organized military expeditions.
- **Craftsmen and Merchants:** Produced goods such as obsidian blades, pottery, textiles, and metal ornaments. Merchants traveled to distant lands, returning with exotic materials.
- **Farmers and Laborers:** Lived in simple homes, grew staple crops like maize and beans. They might have been required to contribute labor to build pyramids or maintain city defenses.

Residential Patterns
Houses usually featured adobe walls and thatched roofs, set around small courtyards. People cooked over open fires, ground maize on stone metates, and stored water in large ceramic vessels. Family altars for household deities could stand in corners of living areas, reflecting a spiritual presence woven into everyday routines.

Local Markets
Tula likely held periodic markets where farmers exchanged produce, potters sold wares, and traders offered goods from remote regions. These events reinforced social bonds and allowed information to flow, connecting Tula with outlying villages.

6.8 The Mythic Quetzalcoatl and Historical Reality

One of the most enduring stories from the Toltec era is the legend of Topiltzin Quetzalcoatl, a priest-king who championed peaceful devotion, banned human sacrifice, and taught advanced skills. According to Aztec accounts, envious rivals forced him into exile. Before departing, he promised to return, a prophecy that later merged into Aztec myths about the arrival of the Spanish in the 16th century.

Symbolic Interpretations
Historians suggest that this narrative reflects real internal power struggles in Tula: perhaps a faction tried to reduce human sacrifice while another wanted to continue it. The exiled king storyline could also be a metaphor for broader cultural shifts. Over time, these events took on a legendary aura, shaping how later peoples viewed the Toltecs.

Aztec Appropriation of Toltec Legacy

The Aztecs saw themselves as heirs to Toltec greatness. They used the term "Toltec" to mean "highly skilled" or "cultured," and claimed descent from Toltec lineages. This claim bolstered Aztec political and religious legitimacy, as it tied them to the glories of Tula and Quetzalcoatl. While we cannot confirm all details of these legends, they show how powerful the Toltec memory became in central Mexican identity.

6.9 Decline of Tula

Tula's prominence lasted roughly until the 12th century CE, after which the city saw unrest and eventual abandonment. Scholars propose multiple reasons for its decline:

1. **Internal Conflicts:** Power struggles between rival factions, possibly connected to religious disputes over the extent of sacrifice.
2. **Environmental or Resource Issues:** Changing climate, over-farming, or depletion of local resources could have strained the city's food supply.
3. **External Threats:** Nomadic or semi-nomadic groups from the north might have attacked Tula, undermining its control over trade routes.
4. **Shifts in Trade Networks:** If Tula's economic advantage eroded due to new trade routes bypassing the city, its wealth and influence would drop, contributing to political instability.

By the mid-1100s or so, Tula was no longer the bustling capital it had once been. Some residents likely stayed behind for a while, but large-scale building projects ceased. The city's ceremonial centers fell into disrepair, and eventually the Toltec heartland faded from prominence.

6.10 Legacy and Influence on Later Cultures

The Toltecs left an enduring mark on the imagination of post-Toltec societies, especially the Aztecs, who dominated central Mexico centuries later. Aztec rulers claimed to be the direct successors of Toltec kings, and they borrowed or adapted much of the Toltec iconography—jaguars, eagles, feathered serpents—for their own state religion and empire-building propaganda.

Artistic and Symbolic Transmission

- **Feathered Serpent Motifs:** Appear in Aztec temples and codices, reflecting the continuing significance of Quetzalcoatl.
- **Warrior Imagery:** The idea of the noble warrior who feeds the gods with sacrificial blood echoes in Aztec ideology.
- **Architectural Features:** Aztec Tenochtitlán had elements reminiscent of Tula's layout, including large pyramids and warrior sculptures (though in different styles).

Historiographical Challenges

Because so much of what we know about the Toltecs comes from Aztec and early Spanish writings produced centuries later, it can be hard to distinguish historical facts from legendary embellishments. Still, archaeology at Tula helps confirm that a powerful city existed there, with advanced building techniques and a wide sphere of cultural influence.

6.11 Summary of the Toltec Epoch

The Toltecs filled a power vacuum in central Mexico after Teotihuacan's fall, forging a robust state focused on Tula. They engaged in trade that brought wealth, created striking warrior-based art, and cultivated a religious framework that made Quetzalcoatl a central figure in their mythology. Despite internal disputes and external pressures leading to Tula's eventual demise, the Toltecs profoundly shaped the region's cultural memory.

Later peoples, especially the Aztecs, elevated the Toltecs as paragons of civilization, skill, and religious devotion—sometimes portraying them as semi-mythical ancestors. Though the Toltecs' true history is more complex and less rosy than the idealized versions, their role in bridging the Classic and Postclassic eras remains crucial. They left a blueprint for military expansion, ceremonial practices, and statecraft that influenced many who followed.

With the Toltecs in decline by the 12th century CE, we move toward new dynamics in central and southern Mexico. The next chapters will address the Mixtecs in post-Classic Oaxaca, the rise of the Aztecs, and the complex interplay of alliances, conquests, and cultural developments that reshaped Mesoamerica leading up to the Spanish arrival.

CHAPTER 7

The Mixtecs and Post-Classic Oaxaca (circa 900 CE – 1521 CE)

During the Postclassic period, the region of Oaxaca saw dynamic changes as various groups vied for power and prestige. The once-prominent Zapotec city of Monte Albán had largely declined, leaving a power vacuum in the highlands and valleys. Into this evolving landscape rose the Mixtecs, known to themselves as the Ñuu Savi, or "People of the Rain." They forged new city-states, developed intricate codices to record their dynastic histories, and engaged in diplomacy, intermarriage, and conflict with neighboring peoples—including the Zapotecs, other Mixtec polities, and eventually the Aztecs.

Below, we will explore how the Mixtecs established themselves in the highlands, how their city-states interacted with one another and with outside powers, and how they recorded their heroic feats and genealogies in richly illustrated books. We will also look at Postclassic Zapotec states, their continued resilience, and how both Mixtecs and Zapotecs confronted the rising might of the Aztec Empire prior to the Spanish arrival.

7.1 The Setting: Highlands and Valleys of Oaxaca

Oaxaca's geography is rugged and diverse, consisting of high mountain ranges, steep valleys, and coastal lowlands. The Mixteca region spans parts of the modern Mexican states of Oaxaca, Puebla, and Guerrero. Here, narrow valleys are separated by mountain ridges, making agriculture challenging yet possible on terraced fields. Rainfall patterns vary, sometimes leading to droughts, so water management is crucial.

Mixtec Heartland

- **La Mixteca Alta (High Mixteca):** Characterized by cooler temperatures and terraced slopes.
- **La Mixteca Baja (Lower Mixteca):** Generally more arid, requiring careful irrigation.

Throughout this terrain, fortified hilltop settlements and smaller farming communities took shape. The fragmentation of the land often resulted in the rise of numerous independent city-states. While some areas had powerful ruling families, no single city ever united the entire region under one banner. Instead, alliances, rivalries, and kinship ties linked these local kingdoms together in a constantly shifting balance of power.

7.2 The Rise of Mixtec City-States

By the 9th or 10th century CE, as Monte Albán's influence faded, Mixtec-speaking groups consolidated in various pockets of the highlands. They built upon earlier traditions—some going back to the Classic period—but introduced new governance structures. Rulers claimed divine or semi-divine rights, often tracing their ancestry to legendary figures mentioned in oral traditions and painted codices.

Key Mixtec Centers

- **Tilantongo (Ñuu Tnoo):** A prominent royal seat linked to legendary rulers such as 8 Deer "Jaguar Claw."
- **Tututepec (Yucu Dzaa):** Located closer to the coastal region, it became a major political force, extending influence over nearby communities.
- **Teposcolula, Coixtlahuaca, and others:** Also rose to significance, each with its own ruling dynasties.

Many Mixtec kingdoms were located on or near defensible hills, where they could protect their people and farmland. Large plaza areas, palaces, and temples provided space for public gatherings, religious rites, and administrative tasks.

Political Organization
Similar to other Mesoamerican cultures, Mixtec rulers (often referred to in Spanish sources as *caciques*) oversaw tribute collection, ceremonial events, and alliances through marriage. Nobles served as local governors, priestly figures, or military captains. Commoners farmed the terraces, produced crafts, and helped build civic-ceremonial structures when the ruler demanded labor.

7.3 Mixtec Codices and Historical Records

One of the most fascinating aspects of Mixtec civilization is the survival of several pictorial manuscripts known as codices, made from deer hide or bark paper. These codices record dynastic histories, battles, marriages, and religious ceremonies using a sophisticated system of pictographic symbols and place signs. Although not fully phonetic like Maya script, Mixtec codices effectively convey stories and genealogies of rulers over many generations.

Famous Mixtec Codices

- **Codex Zouche-Nuttall:** Details the exploits of Lord 8 Deer "Jaguar Claw," a renowned warrior-king whose military campaigns and marriages expanded his power.
- **Codex Vindobonensis (Vienna):** Presents origin myths and genealogies of Mixtec ruling lineages.
- **Codex Bodley, Codex Selden, etc.:** Each captures different historical sequences, sometimes overlapping.

These manuscripts often begin with mythic origins—gods emerging from trees or caves—then transition to more historical events, like the founding of cities or important battles. Marriages between ruling houses are meticulously depicted, since alliances through matrimonial ties were essential for building political coalitions. Nobles and rulers are shown wearing distinctive headdresses or carrying symbols of power, while places are identified by pictorial signs (such as hill glyphs or water glyphs) combined with calendar day names.

Role of the Calendar
Like other Mesoamericans, the Mixtecs used a 260-day ritual calendar and a 365-day solar cycle. Dates in codices appear as combinations of numbers and day signs—for instance, "8 Deer" references the day "Deer" in the 260-day cycle, with the number eight designating which Deer day it was. These names became part of a ruler's identity, linking them to cosmic forces.

7.4 Legendary Figures: Lord 8 Deer "Jaguar Claw" and Lady 6 Monkey

Among the most studied personalities in Mixtec codices are Lord 8 Deer "Jaguar Claw" (8 Deer *Jaguar Claw* in modern reconstructions) and Lady 6 Monkey. Both appear prominently in the Codex Zouche-Nuttall and other manuscripts, and they exemplify how Mixtec rulers used warfare, alliances, and religious authority to expand their domains.

Lord 8 Deer
Said to have ruled Tilantongo, he embarked on military campaigns to subjugate neighboring towns or form alliances with their rulers. His achievements included forging bonds with other noble houses through strategic marriages. However, codices also describe internal conflicts, betrayals, and eventual decline in his fortunes—demonstrating the unpredictable nature of Postclassic politics.

Lady 6 Monkey
A powerful noblewoman featured in some narratives, Lady 6 Monkey held significant agency in forging alliances or legitimizing rulers through ceremonial roles. While many Mesoamerican societies were patriarchal, women of high rank could influence succession, diplomacy, and even warfare outcomes.

These stories highlight how personal ambition, family ties, and religious duties intertwined. They also remind us that Mixtec politics were not simply about kings on thrones but involved aristocratic women who shaped lineage and policy.

7.5 Religion, Ceremonies, and Sacred Geography

Mixtec religion shared broad Mesoamerican concepts, but it also had unique local forms. Sacred places—mountaintops, caves, and springs—were regarded as portals to the divine realm. Ritual specialists or priests performed sacrifices, communicated with ancestors, and interpreted omens tied to the agricultural cycle or political events.

Deities and Ancestors
Mixtec deities frequently appear in codices as anthropomorphic beings associated with rain, wind, or maize. The Rain God (or Rain Deities) was paramount, given the region's dependence on rainfall. Ancestors were also worshiped. Ruling lineages traced their origins to gods or semi-divine heroes, lending a spiritual weight to their claims of authority.

Ceremonies and Sacrifice
Like other Postclassic societies, the Mixtecs practiced bloodletting and, at times, human sacrifice. Victims might be captured warriors or slaves offered during

major dedicatory rites (such as building a new temple). Blood offerings from nobles, including rulers and their spouses, were believed essential to maintaining cosmic order.

Pilgrimage and Offerings
Priests and nobles regularly traveled to shrines located on hilltops or in caves. They brought incense, copal, flowers, and even precious metals or stones as offerings. Some ceremonies took place at boundary markers between city-states, reinforcing political agreements through shared ritual space.

7.6 Postclassic Zapotec States and Interactions

While the Mixtecs gained prominence in the highlands, the Zapotecs continued to inhabit portions of the valleys and surrounding areas. Though Monte Albán was no longer the key center, new city-states emerged, sometimes ruled by local dynasties that claimed descent from earlier Zapotec kings.

Postclassic Zapotec Capitals

- **Zaachila:** Became an important seat of Zapotec power in the central valleys, overseeing a network of smaller towns.
- **Tehuantepec (coastal region):** A strategic port and trading hub, connecting Oaxaca to the Gulf of Mexico and Central America.

Zapotec polities often interacted with Mixtec ones through trade, intermarriage, and warfare. Some alliances were sealed by uniting noble families, while border disputes could lead to skirmishes or longer conflicts. Certain areas with mixed populations saw cultural blending, as both Mixtec and Zapotec languages were spoken, and local elites shared Mesoamerican religious traditions.

Cultural Overlaps

- **Architecture:** Hilltop fortifications, ceremonial plazas, and palace complexes in both Mixtec and Zapotec sites show similarities in layout and design.
- **Writing Systems:** The Zapotec script from earlier epochs influenced Mixtec codices, though the exact degree of interchange is debated.

- **Regional Trade:** Salt, cotton textiles, pottery, and metal goods circulated among Mixtec, Zapotec, and coastal peoples, fostering economic interdependence.

7.7 Warfare, Diplomacy, and Regional Rivalries

Postclassic Oaxaca was far from peaceful. City-states defended their territories fiercely, sought advantageous marriages, and occasionally expanded through conquest. Despite shared cultural traditions, rivalry could be intense.

Fortified Towns
Many communities perched on high ridges with walls or defensive ditches. Watchtowers and gates protected the approach to ceremonial centers. In times of war, peasants might retreat behind fortified lines while armies engaged in battles in the valleys.

Alliance Building
Political marriages served as key tools to avoid prolonged conflict. A Mixtec ruler might marry a Zapotec princess to gain legitimacy in contested zones, or a smaller kingdom might align with a powerful neighbor for protection. The codices often portray lavish wedding ceremonies, with the exchange of jewelry, textiles, and precious objects symbolizing the new bond.

Military Tactics
Warriors used bows, arrows, spears, and obsidian-bladed clubs. Elite soldiers wore cotton armor or carried decorated shields. Captured enemies of high status were typically sacrificed in public ceremonies, reinforcing the victor's prestige.

7.8 Trade Networks and Economic Life

Although warfare was common, trade remained a vital connector throughout Oaxaca and beyond. The region's mountains contained deposits of precious minerals, while valleys produced crops like maize, beans, and chili peppers. Coastal zones offered fish, salt, and even cacao in some places.

Local and Long-Distance Exchange

- **Agricultural Goods:** Maize remained a staple, alongside beans and squash. Surpluses might be traded for craft items.
- **Metals and Stones:** Limited gold and copper deposits in Oaxaca were fashioned into jewelry or ceremonial objects. Turquoise came from farther north via trade routes that stretched into central Mexico.
- **Textiles:** Spinning and weaving cotton or maguey fibers provided clothing and tradeable goods. Skilled weavers made brightly colored garments for nobles.
- **Markets:** City-states likely hosted periodic markets attracting merchants from surrounding regions. Goods were transported by human porters or carried on pack animals (though large-scale use of domesticated animals was uncommon in Mesoamerica, small dogs or turkeys were sometimes used in trade caravans).

7.9 The Aztec Incursions into Oaxaca

Starting in the 15th century, the Aztecs (Mexica) expanded from the Basin of Mexico, seeking tribute and control over strategic regions. Oaxaca's fertile valleys and trade routes proved tempting targets. The Aztecs, under rulers like Moctezuma I and later Ahuitzotl, launched military campaigns southward.

Conflicts and Conquests

- **Mixtec Resistance:** Some Mixtec kingdoms submitted after initial defeats, paying tribute in precious metals, feathers, or foodstuffs. Others fought fiercely, forging alliances with neighboring polities to hold off Aztec incursions.
- **Zapotec Struggles:** The powerful Zapotec kingdom at Zaachila also faced pressure. Some accounts mention alliances between certain Zapotec lords and the Aztecs, ensuring partial autonomy in exchange for regular tribute.
- **Frontier Garrison Towns:** The Aztecs established garrisons near conquered areas, where soldiers could enforce tribute demands and suppress rebellions.

Despite the Aztecs' military might, full subjugation of Oaxaca's highlands was never complete. The rugged terrain, strong local identities, and complex alliance networks prevented total control. However, many Mixtec and Zapotec city-states did pay tribute or recognized Aztec overlords by the late 15th century.

7.10 Cultural Flourishing on the Eve of Spanish Contact

Even under periodic Aztec dominance, Mixtec and Zapotec noble families maintained their traditions, genealogies, and local authority. Artistic production remained vibrant, as seen in surviving jewelry, ceramics, and codices. Temples continued to operate, and festivals honoring local gods or ancestors still punctuated the annual calendar.

Metallurgy and Fine Arts
Gold- and silversmiths in Oaxaca refined intricate metalworking, producing delicate earrings, pectorals, and diadems. Designs often featured stylized animals like jaguars, eagles, or serpents, echoing pan-Mesoamerican symbolism. Skilled potters and lapidary artists created elaborate vessels and carved stones for ritual use or as luxury goods for the elites.

Architectural Remains
Postclassic ruins show modifications to older structures, with new palaces or temple additions. Defensive walls sometimes ringed the entire site, reflecting the unsettled political climate. Decorative friezes and lintels carved with genealogical data or religious motifs speak to the continuing importance of lineage and ritual.

Literacy and Genealogical Memory
The codices maintained an oral-visual record of each city-state's history. Nobles could read these pictorial manuscripts, interpreting place glyphs, day signs, and personal name glyphs. This literacy preserved genealogical continuity, even in times of upheaval. When the Spanish arrived, many codices were unfortunately destroyed or fell into disuse as Catholic evangelization took hold.

7.11 The Spanish Invasion and Its Impact

By the early 16th century, Spanish expeditions ventured into central Mexico. After the fall of Tenochtitlan in 1521, Spanish conquistadors and their Indigenous allies moved into Oaxaca. Some Mixtec and Zapotec rulers surrendered or formed alliances, hoping to retain a measure of autonomy under Spanish rule. Others resisted, but the Spanish, armed with steel weapons, horses, and new forms of warfare, gradually imposed their will.

Early Colonial Restructuring

- **Encomiendas:** Spanish authorities granted control over local labor and tribute to conquerors, disrupting existing tribute relationships.
- **Catholic Missions:** Friars arrived to convert the local population. Many temples were dismantled or repurposed, with churches built on or near sacred sites.
- **Loss of Codices:** Some were burned by zealous priests who saw them as pagan texts. Others decayed over time without proper preservation.

Despite these disruptions, many Mixtec and Zapotec communities adapted, preserving aspects of their languages, crafts, and communal structures. Over the centuries, they blended Indigenous traditions with Catholic practices, creating a distinctive colonial-era culture that still resonates in Oaxaca today.

7.12 Legacy of Postclassic Oaxaca

The centuries leading up to the Spanish conquest were a time of both creativity and conflict. Mixtec and Zapotec city-states continued to evolve, forging ties through marriages, trade, and shared religious practices. Warfare with each other and with the expanding Aztec Empire forced constant shifts in alliances. Yet through it all, local rulers preserved elaborate records of their genealogies, battles, and ceremonial duties in painted codices—an exceptional gift to modern historians and archaeologists.

Enduring Contributions

- **Pictorial Heritage:** Mixtec codices remain some of the most visually striking historical documents from pre-Hispanic Mexico.

- **Metallurgy and Jewelry:** Oaxaca's artisans produced world-class gold and silver work that influenced regional aesthetics.
- **Political and Diplomatic Skills:** Postclassic rulers managed complex alliances and tributes, setting precedents for later Indigenous negotiations under Spanish rule.

Today, the descendants of these groups—modern Mixtec and Zapotec communities—continue to speak their ancestral languages and practice cultural traditions. Their art, festivals, and communal ties maintain a strong sense of identity, linking them to the powerful city-states that once dotted Oaxaca's hills.

CHAPTER 8

The Rise of the Aztecs (circa 1200 CE – 1428 CE)

In the centuries after the fall of Tula and the decline of other Postclassic centers, new powers emerged in the Basin of Mexico. Among these groups were the Mexica, later known as the Aztecs. They arrived as migrants in a region divided among various city-states, including the powerful Tepanecs, Acolhua, and remnants of Toltec-influenced polities. Through a combination of opportunistic alliances, political marriages, and military campaigns, the Mexica transformed themselves from a minor tribe to the founders of the grand city of Tenochtitlan. By the early 15th century, their ambitions would propel them toward forming the Triple Alliance, laying the foundation of the Aztec Empire.

This chapter recounts their legendary origins, the trials they faced on arrival in the Basin of Mexico, and the steps by which they rose to power. We will also explore the early political structures of Tenochtitlan, the role of religion and prophecy in Mexica identity, and how they laid the groundwork for an empire that would eventually dominate much of Mesoamerica.

8.1 Legendary Origins: Aztlan and the Journey South

Aztec (Mexica) lore tells of an ancestral homeland called Aztlan, sometimes depicted as an island paradise in the northwest. The word *Aztec* stems from this mythical place name, though the people called themselves Mexica after one of their tribal deities or heroes. Various codices and later Aztec accounts describe the migratory journey: guided by their patron god, Huitzilopochtli, the Mexica traveled for many years, seeking a promised land where they would become a great people.

Migrant Tribes and Companions
Other groups, such as the Tepanecs, Acolhua, and Xochimilca, also claimed roots in the north or northwest. Over time, these tribes settled around the lakes in the Basin of Mexico—Texcoco, Xaltocan, Chalco, and others. Each group founded small city-states, forging alliances or contesting resources with neighbors.

Arrival in the Basin

When the Mexica arrived, they were seen as crude newcomers by more established city-states. Lacking fertile lands or political connections, they often served as mercenaries or laborers. This subordinate status shaped their early history, compelling them to develop strong martial traditions to gain respect.

8.2 Early Struggles and the Foundation of Tenochtitlan

The Mexica's legendary prophecy stated that they should settle where they spotted an eagle perched on a prickly pear cactus, devouring a serpent. According to tradition, they finally saw this omen on a swampy island in Lake Texcoco. Though the site seemed unpromising at first—marshy land requiring extensive reclamation—it offered natural defenses and direct access to lake resources.

Date of Establishment

Traditional sources give 1325 CE as the founding date of Tenochtitlan. Archaeological evidence suggests the Mexica indeed began building small temples and houses around the early 14th century. Over time, they used chinampa agriculture (floating gardens) to feed their growing population, constructing canals, causeways, and dikes to manage water levels.

Tetzcoco and Other Neighbors

Initially, the Mexica owed tribute or labor to more powerful lords, such as the Tepanec ruler in Azcapotzalco. The Mexica also formed alliances with other city-states or occasionally waged wars on behalf of stronger powers to earn favor. Slowly but steadily, Tenochtitlan expanded, attracting migrants from the surrounding areas who admired the Mexica's fervent devotion to their gods and their martial prowess.

8.3 Huitzilopochtli and Mexica Identity

Central to the Mexica's sense of purpose was the worship of Huitzilopochtli, the god of the sun and war. They believed he had directed them on their journey, shaped their destiny, and demanded blood sacrifice to sustain his cosmic battles against darkness.

Sunrise Warrior

In Aztec cosmology, each dawn was a victory for Huitzilopochtli over the forces of night. To ensure the sun's rebirth, the Mexica offered sacrifices—often captured warriors from rival cities. This practice was not unique in Mesoamerica, but the Mexica placed enormous emphasis on it, integrating warfare and religion into a single driving force.

Priest-Kings

Leaders of Tenochtitlan styled themselves as both political and religious authorities. They performed bloodletting rituals, oversaw temple construction, and organized the distribution of tribute. This dual role reinforced the unity between the state and the divine mission of the Mexica people.

8.4 Political Organization in Early Tenochtitlan

As Tenochtitlan developed, it established a ruling council drawn from noble lineages. The highest position, the *Tlatoani* (speaker), functioned as king. Beneath him were military and administrative officials, each responsible for aspects of governance, such as justice, tribute collection, or foreign affairs.

Calpulli System

The city's neighborhoods were divided into *calpulli*, corporate groups that managed land distribution, local temples, and communal responsibilities. Each *calpulli* provided warriors during campaigns and contributed labor for public works, such as building causeways or temples. This communal structure allowed the Mexica to marshal resources effectively.

Social Hierarchy

- **Nobles (Pipiltin):** Comprised the royal family, priests, high-ranking warriors, and heads of calpulli.
- **Commoners (Macehualtin):** Farmers, artisans, traders. They owed labor to the state and were required to serve in the army.
- **Slaves (Tlacotin):** Generally war captives or debtors. They could sometimes earn freedom under certain conditions.

Even at this early stage, Tenochtitlan displayed a disciplined society, driven by shared myths of destiny and a hunger for expansion.

8.5 Relations with Azcapotzalco and the Tepanec Domination

For much of the late 14th and early 15th centuries, the city-state of Azcapotzalco, under the Tepanec ruler Tezozomoc, held considerable sway over the western side of Lake Texcoco. Tenochtitlan fell under Tepanec influence, paying tribute and providing soldiers for the Tepanec armies. Despite this subordinate status, the Mexica learned warfare strategies and statecraft from their overlords.

Mexica-Tepanec Cooperation
Tenochtitlan benefited from Azcapotzalco's expansions, receiving a share of war spoils and tribute. This arrangement allowed them to grow economically, constructing more temples and palaces. Over time, however, tensions built as the Mexica sought greater autonomy.

Power Struggles
Upon Tezozomoc's death, a succession crisis in Azcapotzalco led to infighting. Sensing an opportunity, the Mexica allied with other disgruntled city-states to challenge Tepanec domination. Among these allies was the Acolhua city of Texcoco, where a young prince named Nezahualcóyotl sought revenge for his father's murder at the hands of the Tepanecs.

8.6 The War of Independence (1426–1428)

The pivotal conflict that enabled the Mexica to break free from the Tepanecs is often called the Tepanec War or the War of Independence. Led by Itzcoatl (r. 1427–1440), the Mexica joined forces with Nezahualcóyotl of Texcoco and other allies to assault Azcapotzalco.

Key Developments

- **Mexica-Acolhua Alliance:** Combined armies laid siege to Azcapotzalco, using canoes to navigate the lakes and causeways.
- **Internal Divisions:** Some Tepanec elites sided with the rebels, weakening Azcapotzalco from within.
- **Capture of Azcapotzalco:** The city fell to the coalition, ending Tepanec hegemony. Victorious Mexica leaders executed hostile lords and claimed control over Tepanec tribute-paying towns.

In 1428, Itzcoatl emerged triumphant. Tenochtitlan was now a rising power, no longer a subordinate tribute-payer. This watershed moment set the stage for the next era of expansion.

8.7 Formation of the Triple Alliance

Following the defeat of Azcapotzalco, Tenochtitlan, Texcoco, and the small city of Tlacopan (also called Tacuba) formed a mutual pact. Known as the **Triple Alliance**, this coalition agreed to share the spoils of conquest—tribute, land, and captive labor. While all three members had a voice, Tenochtitlan soon became the dominant partner, given its strong military and growing economic might.

Tribute Distribution
Conquered provinces often paid goods like maize, beans, cotton, cacao, exotic feathers, and precious metals. The Triple Alliance divided these tributes, with Tenochtitlan typically taking the lion's share. This system enriched the Mexica nobility and financed further campaigns.

Nezahualcóyotl's Role
The Acolhua king, Nezahualcóyotl, re-established Texcoco as a great cultural center. He built palaces, libraries, and gardens. Although Texcoco was overshadowed by Tenochtitlan militarily, its intellectual and artistic achievements contributed to the alliance's prestige.

8.8 Consolidating Power: Early Aztec Expansion

Once free from Tepanec domination, the Mexica wasted no time securing their position. Under Itzcoatl and his successors, especially Motecuzoma I (Moctezuma I), they launched campaigns into surrounding territories, bringing city-states under alliance control.

Key Conquests

- **Coyoacán and Xochimilco:** Neighboring lake cities that had opposed Tenochtitlan were subdued, offering more farmland and controlling key canal routes.

- **Chalco:** A stubborn rival on the southern lakes, eventually defeated after multiple conflicts.
- **Toluca Valley and Beyond:** Gradual expansion westward secured resources and strategic roads.

Victories brought in tribute from newly integrated provinces, feeding Tenochtitlan's urban growth. Skilled artisans, captured from conquered areas, contributed to monumental building projects like the Templo Mayor, the city's main temple dedicated to Huitzilopochtli and Tlaloc.

8.9 Society and Government in the Growing Empire

As Tenochtitlan expanded, its governmental structure became more complex. Military success elevated generals to noble status, while captured tribute financed lavish palace life for the elite. However, certain mechanisms kept the empire cohesive:

Administrative Oversight
Aztec rulers placed local puppet rulers or administrators in conquered provinces to ensure tribute flowed back to the Triple Alliance. In many cases, existing local dynasties were allowed to remain if they pledged loyalty and met tribute quotas. This approach minimized rebellion and leveraged local knowledge.

Merchants (Pochteca)
Long-distance traders, known as the *pochteca*, traveled throughout Mesoamerica, bringing luxury goods—jade, quetzal feathers, precious metals—to Tenochtitlan. They also served as spies, scouting potential regions for conquest. Their wealth and status grew, and they often formed exclusive calpulli, receiving privileges from the throne for their service.

Legal Codes and Education
As the city grew, so did its legal and educational systems. Harsh punishments enforced discipline: theft could result in slavery or death. Elite youths studied at the *calmecac* (school for nobles), learning rituals, statecraft, and warfare, while commoners often attended the *telpochcalli* (youth house) to gain basic military training and vocational skills.

8.10 Religion, Ritual Warfare, and the Concept of the "Flower War"

The Aztecs believed that constant offering of blood was crucial to sustaining the gods. As Tenochtitlan's prestige grew, so did the need for sacrificial captives. Sometimes, neighboring city-states—enemies or even nominal allies—arranged **"Flower Wars."** These were staged conflicts designed to capture prisoners for ritual sacrifice rather than to annex territories.

Purpose of the Flower War

- **Maintain Warrior Ethos:** Ensured a steady flow of trained warriors and tested new recruits.
- **Acquire Captives for Sacrifice:** A central religious obligation, fueling the cosmic balance.
- **Preserve Political Tensions:** By not completely subjugating each other, certain city-states kept a balance of power, avoiding total annihilation.

While these ritual battles might appear less deadly than outright conquests, they still inflicted suffering on local populations and perpetuated cycles of warfare.

8.11 Cultural and Architectural Development

As the Mexica solidified their control over the Basin of Mexico, Tenochtitlan blossomed into a bustling metropolis. Marketplaces overflowed with goods from across Mesoamerica, and grand construction projects symbolized the city's growing importance.

Templo Mayor
This double-pyramid, dedicated to Huitzilopochtli (god of war) and Tlaloc (god of rain), dominated the city's sacred precinct. Expanded multiple times, it showcased elaborate stone carvings, painted reliefs, and altars where priests performed sacrifices. Archaeological excavations in modern Mexico City continue to reveal offerings and sculptures, providing insight into Aztec religious life.

Chinampas
Tenochtitlan's agricultural base hinged on chinampa fields—rectangular plots built up from lake sediment and rotting vegetation. Willow trees planted at the

corners stabilized the chinampas, which produced multiple harvests per year. This method greatly increased food supply, supporting the city's fast-growing population.

Art and Craftsmanship

Stone sculptors, feather workers, and goldsmiths thrived. Aztec art emphasized dynamic imagery of gods, eagles, jaguars, and serpents. Feathers from quetzal or hummingbirds adorned capes and headdresses worn by the nobility. Metal artisans created delicate gold ornaments, sometimes shaped like serpents or flowers.

8.12 Challenges and Rivalries

Despite their success, the Mexica faced ongoing challenges before forming the vast empire known in later chapters. Rival city-states sometimes rebelled, requiring repeated military campaigns. Internal disputes among noble factions could also threaten stability if succession lines became unclear.

Succession Crises

When a Tlatoani died, high nobles and priests convened to choose a successor, typically among the deceased king's relatives. Although such choices were usually uncontested, power struggles could arise if multiple princes or generals had strong claims.

Allied Tensions
Texcoco and Tlacopan occasionally resented Tenochtitlan's dominance in tribute distribution. Carefully managed diplomacy—or displays of force—ensured the alliance remained intact for mutual benefit.

Regional Revolts
Some conquered towns saw an opportunity to rebel if the Aztecs were distracted by other wars. Rapid mobilization of armies was crucial for the Mexica to quell uprisings quickly and deter future insurrections.

8.13 Forging an Empire: Prelude to Greater Expansion

By the early 15th century's close, Tenochtitlan had established itself as a major political and military power. The Triple Alliance model gave it a solid framework for further conquests. Ambitious kings such as Motecuzoma I (Moctezuma Ilhuicamina) and Axayacatl would later push beyond the Basin of Mexico, subduing distant regions and demanding tribute to fuel the empire's constant hunger for resources and sacrificial victims.

Economic Motives
Conquered provinces provided goods impossible to produce locally—cacao from the Gulf Coast, cotton from warmer lowlands, tropical bird feathers from rainforest zones, and precious metals from the south. This influx enriched the noble class and funded grand building projects.

Religious and Ideological Motives
Expansion was framed as a sacred duty, ensuring the supply of war captives for sacrifice. Military success validated the Mexica's divine right to rule and demonstrated Huitzilopochtli's favor. Each victory parade in Tenochtitlan reinforced the population's pride in their city and god.

8.14 Summary of Mexica Ascent

The Mexica's transformation from marginal migrants to dominant rulers of Tenochtitlan is a testament to their resilience and strategic skill. They leveraged alliances, served as mercenaries, and learned from more powerful neighbors like the Tepanecs. Once they defeated their overlords, they quickly established the

Triple Alliance, laying a solid base for the empire-building that would come in subsequent reigns.

Their story intertwines deeply with religious devotion: from the omen of the eagle on the cactus to the daily need for sacrificial blood to sustain the sun. The Mexica harnessed these beliefs to forge a unifying identity that drew thousands of warriors to their cause. Despite the challenges, by the mid-15th century, Tenochtitlan was poised to become the heart of a vast tribute empire.

In upcoming chapters, we will delve deeper into Aztec society and beliefs (Chapter 9) and then follow the Spanish arrival and the dramatic events leading to the fall of Tenochtitlan (Chapters 10 and 11). The Aztecs' rise represents a key turning point in Mesoamerican history—a culmination of centuries of migration, warfare, religious innovation, and cultural exchange that would soon collide with European expansion in the early 16th century.

CHAPTER 9

Aztec Society and Beliefs (circa 1428 CE – Early 16th Century)

The Aztec Empire, forged by the Triple Alliance of Tenochtitlan, Texcoco, and Tlacopan, became one of Mesoamerica's most powerful states in the centuries before Spanish contact. At its core stood the Mexica of Tenochtitlan, whose society blended strong religious devotion, martial discipline, and complex social organization. This chapter explores the many facets of Aztec life: from everyday routines of commoners to grand ceremonies in towering temples. We will learn about their class structures, religious beliefs, economic systems, and artistic achievements, unveiling how these elements combined to sustain the empire's ambitions.

9.1 A Growing Metropolis

By the mid-15th century, Tenochtitlan had transformed from a cluster of swampy chinampas into a thriving city. Raised causeways connected the island to the mainland, facilitating trade and communication. The city's population soared, possibly reaching 200,000 or more by the early 16th century, making it one of the largest urban centers of its time. At Tenochtitlan's heart stood towering pyramids and sprawling palaces that symbolized the Aztecs' strong devotion to their gods.

In these crowded streets and canals, one could encounter farmers bringing fresh produce from chinampas, merchants hawking goods from distant lands, proud warriors adorned in feathered regalia, and priests preparing for the next elaborate ceremony. Meanwhile, the empire grew by conquering neighboring regions, collecting tribute, and imposing its cultural and religious influences on diverse peoples.

The fabric of Aztec life was woven from tradition and adaptation. They borrowed from older Mesoamerican civilizations such as the Toltecs and Teotihuacan, yet they molded these influences into a distinct identity. Their society was at once rigidly hierarchical and surprisingly dynamic. Military accomplishments, patronage by the elite, and merit in specialized roles all shaped how individuals rose or fell within the social order.

9.2 Social Hierarchy: Nobles, Commoners, and Slaves

Aztec society was stratified into clearly defined classes. At the top stood the **pipiltin** (nobles), who held key positions in the government, military, and priesthood. Below them were the **macehualtin** (commoners), who formed the bulk of the population. A separate, smaller group included slaves, known as **tlacotin**, often war captives or debtors who had lost their freedom.

Nobles (Pipiltin)

Nobles inherited their status through birth, though merit could also help certain individuals gain noble rank. They lived in large houses near the ceremonial center, benefiting from tribute and labor collected from conquered provinces. Many nobles served as high-ranking military officers, judges, governors of subject cities, or influential priests. Their privileged position allowed them to wear fine cotton garments and feathers, use luxury items like cacao, and consume special foods not widely available to commoners.

Commoners (Macehualtin)

The majority of Aztecs were commoners, including farmers, artisans, traders, and fishermen. They lived in more modest homes, often made of adobe or woven reeds, typically clustered by extended families. Commoners owed labor and tribute to the state, farmed communal chinampas or fields, and participated in local religious festivals. Skilled artisans—such as potters, weavers, or feather-workers—could gain prestige within their neighborhoods, though they remained socially distinct from the nobility.

Slaves (Tlacotin)

Slavery in Aztec society was not always lifelong nor strictly hereditary. Some individuals sold themselves into slavery to pay off debts, while others were captured in wars. Slaves generally performed manual labor, domestic tasks, or served in the households of nobles. Yet, they retained certain rights. For instance, if a slave escaped from a marketplace and managed to reach the royal palace or a temple without being caught, he could gain his freedom. Also, if a slave married his or her master, they could be freed. This system, while harsh, was more flexible than the rigid chattel slavery seen in other parts of the world at later times.

9.3 The Calpulli System

Beneath the broader social classes lay the crucial foundation of Aztec society: the **calpulli**. A calpulli was a communal group that owned land, maintained a local temple, and served as a fundamental unit of governance and organization.

1. **Communal Land Ownership**
   Each calpulli held farmland in common, distributing plots among its members for cultivation. The produce supported families, and part of it went as tribute to the state or to support community religious ceremonies.
2. **Leadership Structure**
   Each calpulli had a council of elders and leaders who oversaw disputes, arranged communal labor projects, and coordinated tribute payments. They also ensured that religious practices were maintained within the calpulli's own temple or shrine.
3. **Social Support**
   Members of a calpulli often supported one another in times of crisis, pooling resources for funerals, festivals, or to help a family that suffered crop failure. This communal spirit fostered unity and reduced the likelihood of isolated rebellions against state demands.
4. **Military Contributions**
   When the empire mobilized for war, each calpulli was responsible for providing a certain number of warriors. Because of this, strong local identity and pride played a role in motivating soldiers to excel in battle.

The calpulli system provided social stability, as families had both obligations and security through collective resources. Despite the empire's large scale, this smaller communal unit helped Aztecs remain connected to local traditions and responsibilities.

9.4 Family, Gender Roles, and Marriage

In Aztec society, family life revolved around cooperation and strict moral codes. Men and women had defined roles but also shared responsibilities to ensure the household's survival.

Family Structure

Aztec families typically included parents, children, and sometimes grandparents living together. Extended relatives might live nearby, forming tight-knit networks within the same calpulli. Marriage united families economically and politically, with bridewealth or dowries often exchanged. Once married, a couple established their own home but stayed involved with their extended kin for labor and festivities.

Gender Roles

- **Men** were expected to farm, fish, or engage in trade. Many aspired to become warriors, earning honor and a chance to rise in status by capturing enemies in battle. Men typically took part in building projects, paying tribute labor when called upon by local or imperial authorities.
- **Women** oversaw the household, prepared meals, wove cloth, and raised children. Skilled weavers gained prestige, producing cloth for tribute or trade. Women also participated in local religious rites, especially those tied to fertility and household deities.

Yet, Aztec women did not lack influence. Some noblewomen held significant power in court politics or as priestesses. Women could inherit property under certain conditions. Additionally, mothers' roles in moral teaching were highly valued, as they prepared both daughters and sons to uphold Aztec virtues of obedience, piety, and respect.

Courtship and Marriage

Courtship often involved intermediaries, and marriages required parental approval. Feasts, music, and dancing accompanied wedding ceremonies. Marriages could be arranged to seal alliances between families—particularly common among the nobility. While divorce was rare, it was permitted under specific conditions, such as chronic neglect or failure to produce children.

9.5 Education and Moral Codes

The Aztecs believed in educating both noble and common children to instill social values and skills, although their paths diverged based on class.

1. **Calmecac (School for Nobles)**
   Sons (and sometimes daughters) of nobles studied at the *calmecac*, usually attached to a major temple. They learned advanced religious doctrines, rituals, reading basic glyphs, and statecraft. Many students became priests, high-ranking officers, or governmental scribes. Discipline was strict, and self-restraint was taught through fasting, night vigils, and rigorous moral lessons.
2. **Telpochcalli (School for Commoners)**
   Commoner youths attended the *telpochcalli*, found in each calpulli neighborhood. Here, students learned practical skills like farming, basic warfare, and crafts. Morality and respect for elders were emphasized, with teachers instilling obedience to the gods and the empire's laws.
3. **Moral Literature and Teachings**
   Elders passed down moral teachings, often compiled later in written form by post-conquest chroniclers. These teachings, called *huehuetlatolli* ("the sayings of the old"), stressed humility, hard work, honesty, and the importance of communal harmony. They used dialogues and parables to guide youths toward proper behavior as respectful sons, daughters, and future parents or warriors.
4. **Gender-Specific Training**
   Boys practiced weapon handling and learned communal work tasks, while girls received training in household management, weaving, and cooking. However, both boys and girls were taught to revere the gods and uphold the virtues that held Aztec society together.

9.6 Major Deities in Aztec Religion

Central to the Aztecs' worldview was a pantheon of gods who controlled cosmic forces, agricultural cycles, and daily life. Although they acknowledged many deities, a few stood out as principal figures:

1. **Huitzilopochtli (God of War and the Sun)**
   The Mexica's patron deity. They believed he led them from Aztlan to Tenochtitlan. Each day, he battled darkness to bring forth the sun. He demanded blood sacrifices to stay strong, fueling one of the empire's core motivations for expansion and warfare.

2. **Tlaloc (God of Rain and Fertility)**
   Tlaloc governed rainfall, storms, and agricultural bounty. Farmers offered him prayers, small animal sacrifices, and occasional human lives to ensure timely rains. Temples dedicated to Tlaloc often contained water symbols and representations of goggle-eyed figures with fangs.
3. **Quetzalcoatl (Feathered Serpent)**
   A deity associated with wind, learning, and creation myths. Quetzalcoatl was revered by many earlier Mesoamerican cultures (like the Toltecs), and the Aztecs continued his worship. He symbolized wisdom, invention, and the cycle of life and death.
4. **Tezcatlipoca (Smoking Mirror)**
   A powerful, enigmatic god of night, fate, and rulership. Often portrayed as a rival to Quetzalcoatl in mythic stories, Tezcatlipoca demanded strict moral behavior, punishing wrongdoing but also guiding rulers in matters of statecraft.
5. **Xipe Totec (Our Lord the Flayed One)**
   Associated with spring, agricultural renewal, and warfare. His rituals sometimes involved wearing the flayed skin of a sacrificial victim to symbolize rebirth. Despite the grim nature of these rites, they reflected hope for crop regrowth and renewal of life.
6. **Coatlicue (She of the Serpent Skirt)**
   A mother goddess figure, credited with giving birth to Huitzilopochtli. Her imagery in stone sculptures shows her wearing a skirt of entwined snakes, symbolizing fertility, power, and the fearsome aspect of creation.

Each deity had its own festival days, temples, and priesthood. Aztec religion was not monolithic; it evolved over time and absorbed local gods from conquered regions. Tribute-paying cities were often allowed to continue worshipping their ancestral gods, as long as they also recognized the supremacy of Tenochtitlan's deities.

9.7 Rituals, Ceremonies, and Sacrifice

The Aztecs believed the cosmos was in a precarious balance, constantly threatened by chaos. To keep cosmic order, they staged elaborate ceremonies involving music, dance, offerings, and, most famously, human sacrifice. While this practice seems shocking today, for the Aztecs it was a vital religious duty.

Human Sacrifice

1. **Purpose**
   Sacrifice was seen as feeding the gods with precious blood and hearts, ensuring the continuation of the sun's journey and the fertility of crops. Captured warriors from enemy states or volunteers in certain rituals served as sacrificial victims, sometimes treated with reverence before the ceremony.
2. **Methods**
   The most common method involved cutting open the chest on top of a temple pyramid and removing the heart, offered to the deity. Other rites might include decapitation, gladiatorial sacrifice (where a captive fought against multiple Aztec warriors), or being shot with arrows in a ritual dedicated to a particular god.
3. **Scale of Sacrifices**
   Larger festivals could see multiple victims, especially after major military victories. The dedication of the Templo Mayor was recorded as involving thousands of sacrifices in a single multi-day event. Modern scholars debate the exact numbers, but all agree the practice was widespread.

Festivals and Public Participation

Aztecs held a cycle of monthly festivals, each dedicated to specific gods and agricultural milestones. Commoners and nobles alike took part, wearing special costumes, performing dances, and consuming ritual foods. Drums and flutes provided music while priests burned copal incense. The entire city turned out to watch or join in, reaffirming the community's spiritual cohesion.

Personal Offerings and Penances

Not all Aztec ritual life involved grand sacrifices. People made smaller offerings, like paper banners or incense, in household shrines. Self-bloodletting—pricking ears or tongues with a maguey spine—also occurred to offer personal sacrifice to the gods. These acts reminded each individual of their duty to uphold the cosmic order.

9.8 The Templo Mayor and Religious Architecture

At the heart of Tenochtitlan's sacred precinct stood the **Templo Mayor**, a dual pyramid dedicated to Huitzilopochtli and Tlaloc. Its massive stairways led to two distinct temples at the summit. This structure loomed over the city, a visible reminder of Aztec power and piety.

Construction and Expansion

Successive rulers, seeking to outdo their predecessors, rebuilt or expanded the Templo Mayor multiple times. Each layer enclosed the previous version, symbolizing continuity and renewal. Archaeological excavations beneath modern Mexico City have revealed offerings of jade, seashells, obsidian knives, animal remains, and even the bones of exotic creatures—indicating the far-reaching trade networks that supplied dedicatory offerings.

Symbolic Layout

The Templo Mayor's design mirrored Aztec cosmology. One temple was painted with symbols of water and rain for Tlaloc, and the other with war motifs for Huitzilopochtli. This side-by-side arrangement reinforced the balance of forces—agriculture and warfare—that sustained the empire.

Other Temple Complexes

While the Templo Mayor was Tenochtitlan's crowning monument, many additional temples dotted the city: smaller shrines within neighborhoods, altars dedicated to protective gods, and specialized structures for royal funerary rituals. Subject cities also replicated the architectural style, dedicating mini "templo mayor" complexes to their local gods and paying homage to Tenochtitlan's central authority.

9.9 Tribute, Economy, and Daily Sustenance

As the empire expanded, so did its tribute system. Conquered provinces were required to deliver goods on a set schedule—often several times a year. Imperial tax collectors traveled to each region, ensuring compliance and punishing defaulters. These tributes ranged from staple foods to precious luxury items.

Tribute Goods

1. **Foodstuffs:** Maize, beans, chili peppers, salt, and cacao beans.
2. **Raw Materials:** Cotton, tropical hardwoods, feathers from quetzal or other birds, and obsidian for tools or weaponry.
3. **Crafted Items:** Fine cotton garments, woven mats, pottery, jewelry, gold and silver ornaments.

These tributes supplied the Aztec elite and helped feed Tenochtitlan's large population. The surplus also enabled further military campaigns, as it supported professional warriors and financed grand temple dedications.

Currency and Trade

Strictly speaking, the Aztecs did not have a standardized coin-based currency. Instead, they used **cacao beans**, small copper axes, and cotton mantles (called *quachtli*) as mediums of exchange. In local markets, people bartered everyday goods or used cacao beans for smaller transactions—like buying a few avocados or a small piece of pottery.

Agriculture and Chinampas

Tenochtitlan's chinampa system was an agricultural marvel. Narrow, raised garden beds in the shallow lake, chinampas produced multiple harvests per year of maize, beans, squash, amaranth, and other crops. These floating fields sustained the urban populace and reduced reliance on overland shipments. Families passed down chinampa plots through generations, forming valuable property for commoners living near the city's edges.

9.10 The Tlatelolco Market

Tenochtitlan's sister city, **Tlatelolco**, merged with it physically over time but retained a distinct identity. Tlatelolco hosted a massive market—arguably the largest in Mesoamerica—where thousands of vendors gathered daily.

1. **Organization**
   Goods were grouped by type: produce in one sector, pottery in another, textiles and clothing in another. This arrangement helped shoppers find what they needed quickly and allowed traders to compare prices.

2. **Overseers and Judges**
   Market officials kept order, resolved disputes, and ensured fairness in trade. Specialized judges could impose penalties on thieves, fraudulent merchants, or those who disrupted the peace. The Aztecs took market regulation seriously, as it underpinned the city's prosperity.
3. **Diversity of Products**
   A visitor to Tlatelolco's market might see fruit from coastal regions, metal goods from distant mines, live turkeys, domesticated ducks, medicinal herbs, and intricate feather cloaks. Merchants from across Mesoamerica brought their wares, making Tlatelolco a hub of cultural exchange.
4. **Economic Impact**
   The thriving market attracted foreign dignitaries and local consumers alike, contributing to Tenochtitlan's wealth. Pochteca (long-distance traders) often began or ended their journeys here, bringing exotic items—turquoise from the far north, cacao from the southeast, and seashells from coastal regions.

9.11 Cultural Achievements: Art, Poetry, and Codices

While warfare and tribute often dominate narratives of Aztec life, the empire also boasted rich cultural achievements in the arts, literature, and historical record-keeping.

Sculpture and Architecture

Stone masons carved imposing statues of gods, bas-relief panels depicting mythical scenes, and decorative elements for temples. Depictions of serpents, eagles, and jaguars were common, reflecting key symbols in Aztec iconography. Temple facades and palace walls sometimes featured polychrome painting, although much has been lost to time.

Poetry and Song

The Aztecs, especially the nobility, cultivated a tradition of **cuicatl** (poetry and song). These poems celebrated the glory of warfare, lamented life's brevity, or praised the beauty of flowers—metaphors for human existence. Texcoco's ruler, Nezahualcóyotl, was famed for composing philosophical verses questioning fate and mortality. While few original texts survive, later chroniclers recorded fragments of these poems in Roman script after the conquest.

Codices

Aztec codices were screenfold manuscripts made from deer hide or bark paper, painted with bright pigments. They recorded dynastic histories, tribute lists, religious calendars, and ceremonial instructions. Although less textually detailed than Maya hieroglyphs, Aztec glyphs combined pictorial symbols with place names and day signs to convey essential information. Sadly, Spanish authorities destroyed many codices during the conquest, viewing them as pagan documents. Yet a handful survive, offering modern scholars glimpses into Aztec worldview and administrative practices.

9.12 The Aztec Military: Jaguar and Eagle Warriors

The Aztec state was founded on conquest. Military service was a key path to distinction, allowing warriors to ascend socially through successful campaigns and the capture of enemy combatants.

Warrior Societies

Two elite orders stood out: the **Jaguar Warriors** and the **Eagle Warriors**. They wore battle costumes featuring pelts or feathered helmets, symbolizing their fierce and swift nature. Membership required bravery and feats such as capturing multiple foes in battle. Once initiated, warriors gained privileges akin to lesser nobles, including better clothing, land grants, or seats of honor at feasts.

Training and Strategy

Boys in the telpochcalli learned basic military drills from youth. As they matured, they joined campaigns led by experienced captains. The Aztecs fought with obsidian-bladed clubs called **macuahuitl**, spears, bows, and atlatls (spear-throwers). They aimed to wound or stun enemies rather than kill outright, hoping to secure captives for sacrifice. Discipline, combined with strong leadership and religious zeal, often gave Aztec armies an edge against neighboring city-states.

Political Role of Warfare

Conquest fed the empire's tribute system and satisfied the gods' demand for blood. Each new victory validated the ruler's divine right to govern. Elite warriors also functioned as local administrators in conquered territories, ensuring a steady flow of goods and maintaining imperial order.

9.13 Everyday Life and Food

Away from the grandeur of temples and palaces, daily Aztec life centered around the household and the fields. Families rose before dawn to tend crops, spin cotton, or prepare morning meals of **maize tortillas** and beans. Chili peppers provided a spicy flavor to most dishes. Tamales, filled with various meats or vegetables, were another staple. Meat from turkeys, ducks, or occasional game added protein, but most Aztec diets were plant-based.

For refreshment, people drank **pulque** (a mildly alcoholic beverage made from the maguey plant) or **cacao** mixed with water and spices to form a frothy chocolate-like drink. Only nobles, warriors, or merchants with status could regularly afford cacao beverages. Foods like amaranth sweets or honey were treats, enjoyed during feasts and celebrations.

Family bonds and local customs anchored the daily routine. Women shaped the dough for tortillas on stone griddles, known as **comales**, while men might be away fishing, hunting, or on a trading trip. Children fetched water, ran errands, and learned tasks from their parents until they reached an age to attend school.

9.14 Conclusion of Aztec Society and Beliefs

Aztec society was a tapestry of tightly bound communal responsibilities, religious obligations, and imperial ambitions. Through warfare, tribute, and cultural integration, Tenochtitlan grew into a commanding urban center. The empire thrived on a cycle of conquest and ritual sacrifice, believing that sustaining the gods would, in turn, sustain the people.

At the same time, the Aztecs produced remarkable art, refined agricultural systems, maintained bustling markets, and preserved oral and pictorial records.

Their achievements reveal a civilization that balanced order and violence, communal solidarity and rigid hierarchy, spiritual devotion and pragmatic administration.

This complex world—both splendid and harsh—would soon collide with forces from across the ocean. In the next chapter, we will see how European expeditions reached the shores of Mesoamerica, initiating an era of upheaval that would forever alter the course of Aztec and Mexican history.

CHAPTER 10

The Spanish Arrive (Early 16th Century)

As the Aztec Empire stood at the height of its power, a convergence of events across the Atlantic prepared the stage for a transformative encounter. Spain, newly unified under the Catholic Monarchs, was eager to expand its reach, find new trade routes, and accumulate wealth. Christopher Columbus's voyages to the Caribbean in 1492 opened Europe's eyes to the vast potential of lands in the western hemisphere. Explorers, adventurers, and missionaries soon followed, driven by ambition, faith, and sometimes desperation.

In this chapter, we examine the early Spanish expeditions to the Gulf of Mexico, the motivations behind conquest, and the pivotal encounters that set the Aztec world on a path toward irreversible change. Led by figures like Hernán Cortés, the Spaniards would land on foreign shores where political divisions and local resentments against the Aztecs could be exploited. The arrival of these strangers, bearing steel swords and firearms, backed by warhorses and unfamiliar strategies, would forever alter the balance of Mesoamerica.

10.1 Setting the Stage: Europe and the Atlantic World

The early 16th century was a time of transformation in Europe. Following Columbus's voyages, maritime powers such as Portugal and Spain raced to claim new territories and wealth. They sought gold, precious spices, and other resources to fuel their growing economies. Meanwhile, the concept of spreading Christianity to new lands also motivated monarchs and clergy.

Spain's success in the Caribbean—most notably on the islands of Hispaniola and Cuba—brought them gold, sugar plantations, and a labor force in the form of Indigenous people. Yet the Caribbean was only a stepping stone. Rumors of wealthy mainland empires reached Spanish ears, describing cities of gold and advanced civilizations on the continent. Adventurers dreamt of replicating the feats of conquest that had enriched earlier explorers.

10.2 Preliminary Voyages to the Mexican Coast

Before Hernán Cortés's famous expedition, several smaller Spanish voyages skirted the Yucatán Peninsula and the Gulf Coast. These early forays provided glimpses of Maya and other coastal societies but offered no immediate conquest:

1. **Francisco Hernández de Córdoba (1517)**
   Sailing from Cuba, Hernández de Córdoba's expedition reached the Yucatán, making contact with Maya communities. Skirmishes erupted, and many Spaniards were wounded or killed. The survivors returned to Cuba with stories of formidable towns and signs of wealth.
2. **Juan de Grijalva (1518)**
   Grijalva continued exploring the Gulf Coast, traveling as far north as the Pánuco River. He noted populous towns and promising trade prospects. Some Indigenous groups presented tokens of gold and cotton, fueling Spanish hopes of a rich empire inland.

These reconnaissance voyages proved that large, organized societies lay beyond the shoreline. They also returned with Indigenous interpreters and enough intelligence to inspire the next, more ambitious expedition.

10.3 Hernán Cortés: Ambition and Opportunity

Hernán Cortés (1485-1547) was a minor Spanish noble who sailed to the New World seeking fortune. In Cuba, he served under Governor Diego Velázquez, participating in earlier conquests. Cortés was both shrewd and ambitious, eager to command his own expedition. When Velázquez authorized him to lead a journey of exploration in 1519, Cortés immediately began preparing ships, men, and supplies. However, rumors say that Velázquez, wary of Cortés's ambition, tried to revoke the commission at the last minute. Cortés slipped away from Cuba regardless, determined to pursue glory on the mainland.

Cortés's Motives

1. **Personal Glory:** Aspiring to secure wealth and social advancement.
2. **Christian Mission:** Justifying conquest by claiming to spread the Catholic faith.

3. **Imperial Rivalries:** Hoping to stake claims for Spain before other European powers did.

With about 600 men, a handful of cannons, a few horses, and an unshakable resolve, Cortés set sail for the Gulf Coast in early 1519, ready to test his fate in unknown lands.

10.4 The Landing at Veracruz

Cortés and his men arrived near the present-day coast of Veracruz in April 1519. They made contact with local Totonac communities who resented Aztec domination. Upon learning of the Aztecs' tribute demands, Cortés sensed an opportunity to forge alliances with Indigenous groups hostile to the empire.

Founding of La Villa Rica de la Vera Cruz

Cortés formally founded a settlement called **La Villa Rica de la Vera Cruz** (The Rich Town of the True Cross). This act served a legal purpose: by creating a municipal council loyal directly to the Spanish Crown, Cortés bypassed the authority of Governor Velázquez in Cuba. Now, he claimed to act under the King's orders rather than Velázquez's, freeing himself to pursue conquest without interference.

Alliances with Totonacs

In the region around Cempoala, the Totonacs complained about Aztec tribute collectors who demanded heavy taxes and sometimes hostages. Cortés and his lieutenants promised to protect them, forging the first crucial alliance. The Totonacs hoped to free themselves from the Aztecs, while Cortés saw a chance to gain guides, warriors, and local knowledge.

10.5 Malinche (Doña Marina): The Key Interpreter

A pivotal figure in Cortés's success was a young Indigenous woman known as **Malintzin**, or **La Malinche**. Born into a noble family of a Nahuatl-speaking region, she was either sold or captured, eventually ending up among the Maya on the Gulf Coast. When Cortés received her (and other women) from local chiefs, her linguistic skills became apparent—she spoke both Nahuatl (the Aztec language) and Maya dialects.

Role as Interpreter

Initially, Cortés had a Spanish priest named Gerónimo de Aguilar who knew Maya. Malinche would translate Nahuatl to Maya, and Aguilar would translate Maya to Spanish. Over time, Malinche learned Spanish directly, becoming Cortés's primary interpreter, advisor, and intermediary. She conveyed messages, negotiated with Indigenous rulers, and understood the subtleties of Mesoamerican customs.

Historical Debate

Malinche's role remains controversial. Some view her as a "traitor" who aided the Spanish against her own people. Others see her as a survivor making pragmatic choices in a brutal epoch. Regardless, her linguistic and diplomatic abilities were critical to Spanish success, allowing Cortés to navigate the political landscape of central Mexico.

10.6 Burning the Ships: Commitment to Conquest

Once established in Veracruz, Cortés took a bold step to secure his men's loyalty. He ordered most of the ships scuttled or burned (though some accounts suggest they were just run aground). The dramatic gesture signaled that retreat to Cuba was impossible. His soldiers now faced two choices: conquer or perish.

This act, whether wholly literal or partly symbolic, heightened the expedition's unity. Cortés also disciplined any who showed doubts, asserting authority as the sole leader. By removing the option of returning to Cuba, he ensured that the entire company focused on moving inland and confronting the Aztec Empire.

10.7 March Inland: Encounter with the Tlaxcalans

Hearing rumors of a mighty city called Tenochtitlan in the high plateau, Cortés decided to march westward. Along the way, he entered the territory of the **Tlaxcalans**, fierce rivals of the Aztecs who had long resisted subjugation. Initially, the Tlaxcalans fought the Spaniards, testing their metal weapons and warhorses in several skirmishes.

Tlaxcalan Alliance

After bloody battles, the Tlaxcalan elders recognized potential advantages in an alliance with these foreign warriors who opposed the Aztecs. They offered peace, supplies, and more soldiers to help defeat their common enemy. Cortés accepted, forging another vital alliance that would prove decisive in future campaigns.

Tlaxcalan warriors joined the Spanish column, expanding it from a few hundred Europeans to thousands of Indigenous fighters. This show of unity would send a powerful message to other city-states uncertain about the newcomers.

10.8 The Cholula Massacre

From Tlaxcala, Cortés moved toward Cholula, a major religious center allied with the Aztecs. The city was famous for its towering pyramid dedicated to the god Quetzalcoatl. Initially greeted with feasts, the Spaniards heard rumors of an impending ambush by Aztec forces. Whether these rumors were accurate or the result of political manipulation remains debated.

In a preemptive strike, Cortés ordered an attack on Cholula's population. Spanish and Tlaxcalan forces killed thousands, including unarmed nobles and priests. The "Cholula Massacre" served as a grim warning to other cities: any sign of treachery or Aztec allegiance would be met with extreme violence.

This brutal event cemented Cortés's reputation for ruthlessness. It also reinforced the Spaniards' alliance with the Tlaxcalans, who delighted in punishing Aztec allies. The massacre reverberated across central Mexico, instilling fear and uncertainty in the hearts of local rulers.

10.9 Approaching Tenochtitlan

Continuing westward, Cortés and his growing retinue of Spanish and Indigenous troops ascended into the Basin of Mexico. From mountain passes, they caught their first glimpse of the vast lake system and the shimmering island city of

Tenochtitlan. Many were awed by the city's size and beauty: white temple pyramids rising above the water, causeways crossing the lake, and thousands of canoes ferrying goods and people around the canals.

Diplomatic Maneuvers

Moctezuma II (Motecuzoma Xocoyotzin), the Aztec ruler, knew about the Spaniards' approach. He sent envoys bearing lavish gifts of gold, feathers, and textiles, hoping to appease or dissuade Cortés from entering Tenochtitlan. Some historians suggest Moctezuma hesitated, possibly due to prophecies about Quetzalcoatl's return from the east. The Spaniards interpreted the gifts as confirmation of great wealth to be seized.

Conflicting Emotions

As they neared the Aztec heartland, the Spaniards wrestled with both fear and ambition. They had faced stiff resistance in some areas, but also found local allies. Could Tenochtitlan's massive population simply overwhelm them? Conversely, if Moctezuma was uncertain or believed them divine, an opportunity might exist to take the city without immediate bloodshed.

10.10 The Meeting of Cortés and Moctezuma II

On November 8, 1519, Cortés and his forces crossed the causeway into Tenochtitlan. Moctezuma II greeted them with a grand procession of nobles, incense, and elaborate ceremony. Both leaders exchanged courtesies: Cortés offered modest gifts, while Moctezuma presented feathered cloaks, jade, and more gold. Contemporary accounts describe the meeting as highly ritualistic, each side wary yet maintaining a veneer of politeness.

Possible Interpretations

1. **Religious Awe:** Moctezuma might have seen Cortés as linked to divine portents, hence his cordial reception.
2. **Political Calculation:** He could have believed that hospitality was the best tactic to study the invaders before deciding on war or alliance.
3. **Spanish Strategy:** Cortés showed respect but kept his men on alert. He recognized the need to secure the emperor as leverage.

Regardless, the Spaniards found themselves welcomed into the grand palaces of Tenochtitlan—a city more sophisticated than any they had encountered in the New World. For several weeks, they observed Aztec customs, markets, and temples, marveling at advanced engineering and fine arts. All the while, tension simmered, as the empire's leadership tried to assess this small but threatening force in their midst.

10.11 Tensions Build in Tenochtitlan

Despite the initial peaceful reception, distrust grew on both sides. The Spaniards feared an Aztec uprising. Cortés worried about supply lines, the city's overwhelming population, and the precarious loyalty of the local tribes. Aztec nobles questioned Moctezuma's decision to host these intruders who demanded gold, food, and privileges.

Control Over Moctezuma

In a bold and controversial move, Cortés seized Moctezuma and essentially took him hostage within his own palace. This gave the Spaniards a semblance of control, as they forced the emperor to issue orders preventing open rebellion. Though outwardly Moctezuma remained emperor, the empire's real power began shifting into Spanish hands.

Cultural Clashes

Spanish soldiers, driven by Christian zeal, desecrated some Aztec idols, shocking local priests and citizens. Rumors of sacrifices and deeper Aztec plots against the newcomers circulated among Spanish ranks. Meanwhile, many Aztecs seethed at the humiliating spectacle of their ruler being manipulated by outsiders. A confrontation seemed inevitable unless events took another turn.

10.12 Prelude to Conquest

In the coming months, the situation in Tenochtitlan would spiral into violence. The Spaniards' hold on Moctezuma could not last indefinitely, and discontent among Aztec warriors grew. The arrival of additional Spanish forces from Cuba—intent on arresting Cortés—complicated matters, leading Cortés to leave

Tenochtitlan briefly. In his absence, tension erupted into open conflict, culminating in a dramatic siege and the eventual fall of the city.

But at this juncture—late 1519 into early 1520—none could have predicted the full scale of destruction that awaited Tenochtitlan. The Spanish had arrived, forging alliances, sowing division, and capturing the Aztec emperor without fully grasping the resilience and unity that could still emerge from the populace. Disease, weaponry, and indigenous alliances would all play decisive roles in the next phase of the conquest story.

CHAPTER 11

The Conquest of Tenochtitlán (1520 – 1521)

By early 1520, Spanish forces under Hernán Cortés were stationed in the Aztec capital of Tenochtitlán, having taken Emperor Moctezuma II hostage. The tension in the city was palpable. Aztec nobility chafed under foreign demands for gold and tribute, while ordinary residents were outraged by cultural offenses—especially attacks on sacred idols—perpetrated by some Spaniards. Many felt Moctezuma had failed to defend the city's dignity. Meanwhile, Cortés was distracted by internal threats: soldiers sent from Cuba to arrest him and the delicate alliances he'd formed with Tlaxcalans and others resentful of Aztec rule.

In this pivotal chapter, we will follow the events that triggered the eruption of violence in Tenochtitlán, leading to the Spanish and their allies fleeing the city under desperate circumstances. We will see how disease, politics, and sheer human resilience shaped the final siege that ended in the empire's downfall. Though this conquest is one of the most famous episodes of the Spanish incursion into the Americas, it is also a story of alliances among Indigenous polities, conflicting leadership among the Aztecs, and the transformative power of epidemic disease.

11.1 Rising Tensions and the Death of Moctezuma II

The Arrival of Pánfilo de Narváez's Forces

While Cortés maneuvered to keep a hold over Tenochtitlán, Governor Diego Velázquez of Cuba dispatched **Pánfilo de Narváez** with a larger force to apprehend Cortés and reassert Velázquez's authority. Narváez landed on the Gulf Coast, threatening to undermine everything Cortés had achieved. Facing this new threat, Cortés made the risky decision to leave a smaller contingent in Tenochtitlán under the command of Pedro de Alvarado, while he led most of his troops to confront Narváez.

Cortés's sudden departure meant fewer Spaniards remained to hold the Aztec emperor captive. Moctezuma's ability to control restive nobles eroded, and

Alvarado's leadership style quickly proved controversial—he lacked Cortés's diplomatic finesse and was more prone to overreaction.

The Massacre at the Festival of Toxcatl

During Cortés's absence, Aztec nobles organized the annual **Toxcatl** festival honoring the god Tezcatlipoca. They had received Alvarado's permission to hold the ceremony in the city's sacred precinct. Dressed in elaborate regalia, dancers and priests gathered for rituals. However, Alvarado became suspicious that the Aztecs were planning an attack on the Spanish garrison during the festivities, although modern historians debate whether these suspicions had any basis in fact or were the result of fear and misinterpretation.

Acting on his fears, Alvarado and his men suddenly attacked the unarmed celebrants in the temple courtyard, killing many nobles and priests. This unprovoked massacre ignited fury throughout Tenochtitlán. Citizens rose against the Spanish, besieging their quarters and cutting off their food supplies. Alvarado's rash decision destroyed any remnants of goodwill that might have lingered.

Cortés Returns

Having defeated Narváez on the coast—using strategic cunning rather than outright numbers—Cortés convinced many of Narváez's troops to join him, lured by promises of wealth in the Aztec capital. He then raced back to Tenochtitlán to rescue Alvarado's detachment. Upon arrival, Cortés found the Spanish barricaded in their palace compound, under constant Aztec attack.

He attempted to restore order by instructing Moctezuma to calm the crowds. Yet by this time, the emperor's authority was nearly gone. Some accounts claim that when Moctezuma tried to speak from a balcony or rooftop to quell the mob, he was met with stones and arrows—possibly mortally wounding him. Spanish sources suggest he died from these wounds; Aztec chronicles and later interpretations sometimes accuse the Spaniards of killing Moctezuma themselves. Either way, his death symbolized the collapse of the old order in Tenochtitlán.

11.2 The Noche Triste (Night of Sorrows)

Cuitláhuac's Leadership

After Moctezuma's death, the Aztec nobility selected **Cuitláhuac**—a capable and determined leader—as the new emperor. Under Cuitláhuac's command, Aztec forces escalated attacks on the Spanish within the city, cutting off causeways and controlling waterways. Cortés realized that if he and his men stayed, they risked annihilation. They decided to attempt a stealthy night escape.

Attempting to Flee

On the rainy night of June 30, 1520, the Spaniards and their Indigenous allies tried to slip out of the city via the **Tlacopan causeway**. They carried as much gold as they could loot from the royal palaces, greed fueling their departure. Aztec warriors, however, were alert. They spotted the escaping columns and sounded the alarm. Fierce fighting erupted in the dark. Canoes approached from the lake, archers peppered the Spaniards with arrows, and foot soldiers charged from behind.

The chaos forced many Spaniards into the canals where they drowned under the weight of stolen gold. Others were captured or killed on the causeway itself. Cortés, wounded, managed to cross with some survivors, but the losses were staggering. Spanish sources name this escape **La Noche Triste** ("The Night of Sorrows"), for the despair that followed. Those who survived regrouped outside the city, numb at the scale of the disaster.

Aftermath of the Night Escape

Cortés's once-confident force had been devastated. Horses, cannons, and hundreds of men were gone. Even loyal Indigenous allies, like the Tlaxcalans, suffered heavy casualties. The flight also broke much of the Spanish aura of invincibility. Yet, Aztec forces had not fully annihilated the enemy. Cortés's cunning and luck, combined with a measure of resilience, would soon allow the Spanish to rebuild.

11.3 Reorganization and the Spread of Disease

Retreat to Tlaxcala

Cortés led the survivors on a hazardous march to **Tlaxcala**, pursued by Aztec warriors along the way. In at least one major skirmish, the Battle of Otumba, the Spaniards faced a large Aztec force. They barely escaped after Cortés reportedly killed a high-ranking Aztec commander, causing confusion among the enemy. Ultimately, the battered group reached Tlaxcalan territory, where they recuperated. The Tlaxcalans, despite having lost many warriors themselves, decided to maintain their alliance with Cortés—still seeing him as their best hope to topple the Aztecs once and for all.

Smallpox Epidemic

Around this same time, a catastrophic **smallpox epidemic** swept through central Mexico. The disease likely arrived with a Spanish slave who accompanied Narváez's expedition. Indigenous communities had no immunity to Old World illnesses. The virus spread rapidly through Tenochtitlán and surrounding areas, decimating the population. The Aztecs referred to smallpox as a plague of painful pustules that left survivors scarred—if they survived at all.

The epidemic struck at the heart of Aztec society, killing farmers, artisans, warriors, and even leaders. Emperor Cuitláhuac himself succumbed to the disease after ruling for only a few months. This vacuum of power was filled by **Cuauhtémoc**, Moctezuma's nephew, who became the next Aztec tlatoani (ruler). But the empire was severely weakened, with entire neighborhoods and towns left partially abandoned or in disarray.

11.4 Preparations for the Final Siege

Cortés's New Allies and Armaments

In Tlaxcala, Cortés reorganized his forces. His personal force was replenished by reinforcements from Cuba, as well as many ex-Narváez soldiers. He oversaw the construction of **brigantines**—small, maneuverable ships designed for lake warfare. These were built in sections, transported overland, and reassembled near the lake of Tenochtitlán.

Simultaneously, Cortés strengthened alliances with other city-states around the Basin of Mexico, many of which resented Aztec tributary demands or had rivalries with Tenochtitlán. These states hoped to gain advantage or independence by siding with the Spaniards. With each new ally, Cortés gained local knowledge, warriors, and supply routes to support the coming assault on Tenochtitlán.

Aztec Preparations and Cuauhtémoc's Leadership

Despite staggering population losses, Tenochtitlán's defenders readied themselves under Cuauhtémoc's firm leadership. They repaired causeways, fortified city walls, and prepared canoes to attack any Spanish brigantines. Priests performed rituals to encourage the warriors and petition the gods for deliverance from the foreign invaders. There was a sense of unity in the face of devastation: having seen the cruelty of the Spaniards and the ravages of disease, many in Tenochtitlán believed they had no choice but to fight to the end.

11.5 The Siege of Tenochtitlán

Encirclement by Land and Water

In the spring of 1521, the Spanish-led coalition moved to encircle Tenochtitlán. Cortés positioned his brigantines on the lake, aiming to disrupt Aztec canoe traffic and block supplies. On land, Spanish forces and thousands of Indigenous allies occupied the main causeways: **Tepeyacac** (to the north), **Tlacopan** (to the west), and **Iztapalapa/Churubusco** (to the south). They advanced gradually, seizing outlying neighborhoods or towns.

Cortés directed coordinated attacks, with brigantines supporting land units by bombarding canoes or shore positions. Aztec warriors launched night raids, using their superior knowledge of the canals. Civilians inside Tenochtitlán suffered from hunger and thirst as the siege tightened, fresh water supplies became contaminated, and farmland was lost.

Fierce Street-by-Street Fighting

Eventually, Spanish and Tlaxcalan forces breached the city's outer defenses. The battle descended into brutal street fighting. Houses were burned or toppled to prevent the Aztecs from using them as defensive positions. Every canal crossing was contested. Aztec warriors often feigned retreats, luring Spaniards and allies into ambushes. Meanwhile, disease and starvation took their toll on both sides. Still, the Spanish had a technological edge: steel swords, gunpowder-based firearms, crossbows, and the unwavering support of numerous Indigenous allies who wanted Tenochtitlán subjugated.

Psychological Warfare

Cortés also used psychological tactics. He had captured Aztec nobles or priests publicly display the hopelessness of resistance, hoping to demoralize the city. Some negotiations for surrender were attempted, but Cuauhtémoc refused. The Aztec spirit to defend their sacred city was strong, even amidst the dire circumstances.

11.6 Fall of the Aztec Capital

Destruction of Tlatelolco

As the siege wore on, the defenders fell back toward the Tlatelolco district in the northern section of the island. Houses were filled with the sick and wounded, and corpses floated in the canals. Food became scarce, forcing many to eat anything available. By August 1521, Spanish and allied forces had effectively cut Tenochtitlán in half. Fighting continued around the sacred precinct, but the city's capacity to resist was collapsing.

On August 13, 1521—sometimes marked as the official end date of the Aztec Empire—Cuauhtémoc was reportedly captured while attempting to flee in a canoe. Once the emperor was seized, organized resistance quickly ended. The remaining defenders surrendered or were killed. The final days saw scenes of devastation, with entire neighborhoods in ruins. The once-magnificent city was left in a state of rubble and disease.

Aftermath for Survivors

Thousands of Aztec civilians died from hunger, smallpox, or direct violence. Survivors faced an uncertain future. Many were enslaved or forced into tributary labor for the Spanish. Temples were dismantled, idols smashed, and efforts began to transform Tenochtitlán into a new Spanish capital: soon to be called **Mexico City**. Though fighting continued in outlying regions and among other Indigenous polities, the fall of Tenochtitlán marked a decisive moment, signaling Spanish ascendancy in central Mexico.

11.7 Legacy of the Conquest

Human and Cultural Loss

The conquest of Tenochtitlán is often described as one of history's most dramatic military campaigns. Beyond the warfare itself, smallpox and other epidemics devastated the local population. Artwork, religious traditions, and structures were dismantled or repurposed for Catholic churches. Many codices, which detailed Aztec history and knowledge, were destroyed, erasing centuries of intellectual heritage.

Yet despite these losses, Aztec cultural elements persisted. Surviving noble families adapted to the new order, bilingual interpreters mediated everyday governance, and many aspects of Indigenous social life continued covertly. The city's canals, chinampas, and market traditions influenced how the new Spanish city functioned, even as conquerors tried to impose their own architectural style and administrative systems.

A Network of Allies

Though often portrayed as a clash between Spaniards and Aztecs, the conquest was equally about alliances among Indigenous peoples. Without Tlaxcala and other Indigenous groups who rebelled against Tenochtitlán, Cortés's victory might have been impossible. This pattern—turning local resentments into a coalition—became a hallmark of Spanish conquests elsewhere in the Americas.

Cuauhtémoc's Fate

After the city fell, Cuauhtémoc was initially kept alive, though under Spanish control. Cortés forced him to provide gold or reveal hidden treasures, culminating in allegations of torture. Cuauhtémoc denied knowing where additional gold was hidden, and Cortés grew frustrated with the meager loot. The last Aztec ruler later accompanied Cortés on expeditions to other parts of Mesoamerica, only to be executed on suspicion of plotting a rebellion. Cuauhtémoc's final stand and his dignity in facing defeat later transformed him into a symbol of Indigenous resistance and identity.

11.8 Summary of the Conquest

The conquest of Tenochtitlán was a complex event shaped by:

1. **Spanish Ambition and Ruthlessness:** Cortés's strategic moves, the alliances he forged, and his willingness to use force, deception, and negotiation.
2. **Indigenous Rivalries and Alliances:** Tlaxcalans, Totonacs, and other city-states joined the Spanish to break free from Aztec hegemony.
3. **Disease:** Smallpox ravaged the densely populated Aztec heartland at a crucial moment, thinning defenses and undermining leadership.
4. **Military Technology and Strategy:** Steel weapons, cavalry, and cannons gave the Spanish an advantage in open battle, while brigantines controlled lake approaches.
5. **Internal Political Shifts:** Moctezuma's weakening hold on power, the brief rule of Cuitláhuac, and then Cuauhtémoc's brave but ultimately unsuccessful defense.

By mid-August 1521, Tenochtitlán had fallen, ushering in a new era of Spanish rule in central Mexico. While some remote regions and other cultures continued to resist, the Aztec capital's collapse symbolized the end of one of Mesoamerica's greatest empires.

CHAPTER 12

Early Colonial Rule (1521 – Late 16th Century)

With Tenochtitlán in ruins and the Aztec Empire effectively dismantled by 1521, Spain embarked on a new phase of domination in central Mexico. Soldiers who had fought for conquest now sought titles, land, and the labor of Indigenous communities. Hernán Cortés, riding the waves of victory, strove to shape a colonial government under the distant oversight of the Spanish Crown.

In this chapter, we will explore how Spanish colonial structures took root in the immediate aftermath of conquest, how the Catholic Church became a central force in reshaping Indigenous societies, and how everyday life changed for both conquerors and conquered. Although the Spanish aimed to replicate European feudal models, Indigenous communities often adapted these new systems to preserve aspects of their traditions. Through violence, negotiation, and cultural blending, the early colonial period set the stage for the complex society that would emerge as New Spain.

12.1 Aftermath of the Conquest

Cortés as Governor and Captain General

Immediately after Tenochtitlán's fall, Cortés declared himself the head of a provisional government. Seeking official validation, he corresponded with King Charles V of Spain, describing the wealth and potential of the newly subjugated territory. By 1522, the Crown recognized him as **Governor and Captain General of New Spain**. However, Spanish royal authorities remained cautious of letting any single conquistador gain too much power, setting the stage for future conflicts between the Crown and colonial officials.

Rebuilding Mexico City

Cortés ordered the construction of a new city atop the ruins of Tenochtitlán. Canals were filled or rerouted, Aztec temples were razed, and Spanish-style buildings began rising. Stones from dismantled pyramids were reused in churches and government offices. Nevertheless, some remnants of the Aztec city—particularly the lake environment and chinampa agriculture—persisted. Within a few years, **Mexico City** took shape as the capital of New Spain, serving as a base for further expeditions into the hinterlands.

Indigenous Population Decline

In addition to the recent losses from warfare and smallpox, further epidemics—measles, typhus, and others—continued ravaging Indigenous populations. Scholarly estimates suggest up to 80-90% population decline in some regions within the first century of colonial rule. Entire towns vanished, while survivors regrouped or migrated. This demographic catastrophe reshaped labor systems and fueled competition among Spanish settlers for Indigenous workers.

12.2 The Encomienda System

Origins and Purpose

To reward conquistadors and ensure they had access to labor, the Spanish Crown introduced the **encomienda** system. In theory, an encomienda was a grant of responsibility over a certain Indigenous community, allowing the encomendero (holder of the grant) to collect tribute—often in the form of labor, crops, or goods. In return, the encomendero was supposed to protect the Indigenous people and ensure their Christian instruction.

Reality of Exploitation

In practice, encomenderos often abused their privileges, forcing long hours of labor and exacting heavy tribute. Many Indigenous communities suffered under these demands, particularly amid widespread disease and famine. Although the Crown and religious orders tried to moderate abuses through regulations, local oversight was weak. Encomenderos, eager to enrich themselves, typically pushed communities to or beyond their limits.

Over time, the Crown grew wary of powerful encomenderos who might form a new aristocracy in the Americas, undermining royal authority. Debates ensued regarding how to limit or reform the system. Nevertheless, encomiendas remained a cornerstone of early colonial economics for decades, allowing Spanish settlers to extract wealth from Indigenous labor.

Impact on Indigenous Communities

For Indigenous families, encomienda tribute obligations could mean farming Spanish crops, mining silver or gold, or working on distant haciendas (large estates). People struggled to maintain their own subsistence activities alongside forced labor. Some communities resisted or fled to remote areas; others negotiated partial accommodations, forging new local leadership structures recognized by the Spanish in exchange for stable tribute flows.

12.3 Role of the Catholic Church

Missionary Efforts

From the earliest stages of conquest, Franciscan, Dominican, and Augustinian missionaries arrived to evangelize the Indigenous populace. They built **mission churches**, taught basic Christian doctrine, and often learned local languages to communicate more effectively. Missionaries also opposed some encomendero abuses, seeing themselves as protectors of Indigenous souls.

Indigenous leaders, especially those who survived the upheavals, sometimes converted to Christianity for practical reasons—aligning themselves with the new colonial order to secure a measure of autonomy. As missions spread, they established schools and hospitals, inadvertently becoming important community centers.

Conversion and Syncretism

While colonial authorities aimed to eradicate "idolatry," many Indigenous beliefs persisted. A process of **syncretism** emerged, where elements of Christian worship merged with Indigenous traditions. For instance, festival dates sometimes coincided with older ritual calendars, and local saints might inherit attributes of pre-Hispanic gods. The church might stand atop an old temple site, yet local people would bring offerings reminiscent of older rites.

This blending of beliefs was not always sanctioned by Spanish clergy, but it proved impossible to stamp out Indigenous religious expressions entirely. Over generations, Catholicism in New Spain took on distinctly local flavors, with devotion to specific saints, Marian apparitions, and processions that echoed older communal ceremonies.

12.4 Establishing Colonial Institutions

Audiencias and Viceroyalty

The Spanish Crown created administrative bodies called **audiencias** to oversee governance and justice in New Spain. The first Audiencia of Mexico was established in the 1520s, led by a group of judges known as oidores. However, corruption plagued early audiencias, as some officials abused power or colluded with encomenderos.

To centralize authority, the Crown eventually instituted the **Viceroyalty of New Spain** in 1535, appointing **Antonio de Mendoza** as the first viceroy. The viceroy acted as the king's representative, supervising regional governance, finances, and legal matters. Over time, this viceroyal system expanded to include territories far beyond the former Aztec realm, encompassing much of North and Central America, the Caribbean, and the Philippines.

Municipal Councils (Cabildos)

Spanish towns established **cabildos** (municipal councils) responsible for local administration—managing markets, policing, and local public works. Wealthy settlers or encomenderos often dominated these councils, using political power to shape tribute collection and labor systems. Indigenous communities, meanwhile, had their own local councils recognized by Spanish law to some extent, led by **gobernadores** (local governors) or **caciques** (traditional chiefs).

Although subordinate to Spanish overlords, these Indigenous councils played a key role in negotiating day-to-day demands. They collected tribute and relayed official decrees, but also tried to preserve aspects of their pre-conquest social structures. Over time, the interplay between Spanish cabildos and Indigenous councils formed the bedrock of colonial local governance.

12.5 The Emergence of a Colonial Economy

Agriculture and Ranching

As Spanish settlers established estates, they introduced European crops such as wheat, sugarcane, and new livestock like cattle, sheep, and horses. These transformed the landscape around Mexico City and in fertile valleys. Large ranches, or **estancias**, emerged for raising livestock, while **haciendas** cultivated wheat or sugar for local consumption and export. Overgrazing sometimes disrupted Indigenous agriculture, leading to soil depletion and conflicts over land use.

Mining

Mining quickly became another pillar of New Spain's economy. Although Cortés's men initially sought gold, large-scale **silver** mines were discovered in regions like **Zacatecas** and **Guanajuato**. These areas boomed as Spanish entrepreneurs and Crown officials invested in extracting silver, which fed Europe's appetite for precious metals. Indigenous labor, often coerced through the **repartimiento** system (a forced labor draft), sustained the mines. Conditions were harsh, with long hours underground leading to accidents and illness.

Trade Networks

Ports on the Gulf of Mexico and the Pacific facilitated transatlantic and transpacific trade. **Veracruz** linked New Spain to Seville in Spain, shipping silver and other goods, while importing European textiles, weapons, and sometimes African slaves. On the Pacific side, **Acapulco** served as a key port for the Manila Galleon trade with Asia, bringing silk, spices, and other luxury items. Mexico City, as the colonial capital, became a hub where goods from all directions converged.

Indigenous communities found new opportunities in these markets, selling woven textiles, pottery, or agricultural products. Some even adapted to raising European livestock. However, profits mostly flowed to Spanish elites or the Crown. A new social stratification emerged, with Spaniards and those of mixed ancestry often controlling commerce, while most Indigenous people remained at the bottom of the economic ladder.

12.6 Social and Racial Hierarchies

The Casta System

A complex **casta** (caste) hierarchy developed as Spaniards intermarried or had children with Indigenous women, and eventually with people of African descent. This system categorized individuals by racial background: **peninsulares**

(Spaniards born in Spain) ranked highest, followed by **criollos** (Spaniards born in the Americas), **mestizos** (mixed Spanish-Indigenous), **mulattos** (mixed Spanish-African), **zambos** (mixed African-Indigenous), and so on, with Indigenous and African peoples often occupying the lowest social positions.

Though fluid in practice, these categories influenced one's access to education, priesthood, and government positions. Peninsulares and high-ranking criollos held the top roles, while mestizos found limited upward mobility if they acquired wealth or patronage. Indigenous communities, despite numeric predominance, were placed in a separate category under Spanish protection but heavily taxed and restricted.

Daily Interactions and Cultural Blending

In many towns, Indigenous, Spanish, African, and mixed-race populations interacted daily—trading, laboring side by side, or even living in the same neighborhoods. Over time, cultural exchange became inevitable. Clothing styles blended Indigenous textiles with European cuts, religious festivals combined Catholic and local elements, and culinary traditions merged old and new world ingredients (maize, chili peppers, wheat, sugar, etc.). The line between classes sometimes blurred, especially in frontier regions or small communities where personal relationships overshadowed formal casta labels.

12.7 Indigenous Adaptations and Resistance

Legal Strategies

Indigenous elites, such as **caciques** or former noble families, frequently used the Spanish legal system to defend their lands, negotiate tribute levels, or protest abuse by encomenderos. They brought lawsuits before audiencias, appealed to the viceroy, and sometimes wrote petitions to the King. Mission-educated scribes helped craft these documents in Spanish, combining formal legal arguments with references to local custom.

While success varied, the fact that Indigenous communities adopted Spanish legal procedures demonstrates their resilience and adaptability. Over time, a body of colonial law—**derecho indiano**—grew around such cases, reflecting a patchwork of Crown decrees and local realities.

Armed Rebellions

Not all Indigenous resistance took peaceful forms. Some communities rose in open revolt against tribute burdens or forced labor. One of the early notable rebellions involved the **Maya** in the Yucatán, though it took the Spanish decades to fully subdue them. In central Mexico, pockets of resistance flared sporadically, but widespread rebellion was rare, partly because disease had severely reduced populations and many local leaders found it more advantageous to negotiate than to fight.

Religious Persistence

Even as missionaries established Catholic churches, many Indigenous people continued to venerate ancestral deities or local spirits in secret. Ritual dances, cures by shamans, and veneration of cave or mountain shrines carried on discreetly. In some places, the church hierarchy tolerated "harmless" local customs if they helped bring people into Catholic festivals. Yet more direct forms of "idolatry" could be harshly punished if discovered, particularly by zealous friars or the Inquisition.

12.8 The Friars and Education

Building Schools and Convents

Religious orders—Franciscans, Dominicans, Augustinians—constructed **convents** (known as conventos) and monasteries across New Spain. They served as centers of religious instruction, charity, and often rudimentary education. Some friars worked tirelessly to learn Indigenous languages, producing catechisms, dictionaries, and grammar books to facilitate conversion and teaching.

Mission schools provided instruction in reading, writing, and Catholic doctrine. Noble Indigenous youths were sometimes singled out for advanced training, so they could help spread Christian teachings among their own communities. This approach had mixed results, but it led to a generation of bilingual Indigenous scribes and local church functionaries who mediated between Spanish officials and their own people.

Cultural Contributions

Ironically, some friars became the best chroniclers of pre-Hispanic cultures. Figures like **Bernardino de Sahagún**, a Franciscan friar, collaborated with Indigenous students to compile the **Florentine Codex**, documenting Aztec language, religion, history, and customs in great detail. While the friars aimed to catalogue these beliefs to refute them, their work preserved invaluable records of Mesoamerican traditions that might otherwise have been lost.

12.9 Transformations in Everyday Life

Food and Housing

Spanish colonial towns featured a central plaza flanked by a church and government buildings. Wealthy Spaniards built stone houses with interior courtyards, while many Indigenous families continued living in simpler adobe or wattle-and-daub structures. Over time, new architectural styles mixed with local building techniques.

Foodways changed as well. Corn tortillas, beans, and chili peppers remained staples for Indigenous and many mestizo households. Europeans introduced wheat bread, pork, beef, cheese, and sugar, which became more common among the upper classes. Over centuries, this blending gave rise to new "Mexican" cuisines—moles, tamales with pork or chicken, sweet breads, and so on.

Clothing and Textiles

European clothing like breeches, dresses, and shoes gradually spread, though many Indigenous people continued wearing traditional garments. Cotton production expanded for clothing. Skilled Indigenous weavers adopted Spanish looms, producing hybrid textile designs. Over time, certain garments like the **huipil** (a traditional blouse) or the **rebozo** (a shawl) blended Indigenous motifs with Spanish-influenced patterns, reflecting colonial-era fusion.

12.10 The Emergence of a New Social Order

As the 16th century progressed, New Spain took on a distinct character. Spain's tight control over Atlantic trade routes, combined with the silver boom, made the colony profitable. A growing class of **criollos** (American-born Spaniards) began to develop local interests. Mestizos increased in number, serving in roles ranging from artisans and shopkeepers to junior clergy or minor administrative posts. Despite these changes, peninsulares and high nobility dominated high offices well into the colonial era.

Indigenous polities that cooperated with the Spanish—like Tlaxcala—received certain privileges, though they also faced new burdens. Meanwhile, enclaves of Afro-descendant communities formed from enslaved Africans brought to work on sugar plantations or in domestic service. The cultural tapestry of New Spain thus became increasingly complex, layering Spanish institutions on top of vibrant Indigenous traditions, with African influences adding another dimension.

12.11 Challenges to the Encomienda System

The "New Laws" and Las Casas

As reports of encomienda abuses spread, advocates like **Bartolomé de las Casas**, a Dominican friar, pleaded with the Crown to protect Indigenous peoples. Las Casas wrote passionately about the violence and exploitation he witnessed, describing the brutalities inflicted on Native communities. Partly in response, the Crown issued the **New Laws of 1542**, which aimed to limit the power of encomenderos by making encomiendas non-hereditary and requiring better treatment of Indigenous subjects.

However, many encomenderos resisted these reforms, leading to rebellions in places like Peru. Though the New Laws were not fully enforced, they foreshadowed the gradual transition away from encomienda labor toward other systems of colonial exploitation, such as **repartimiento** (temporary labor drafts) and eventually wage labor on haciendas.

Shift Toward Haciendas

Over time, wealthier settlers began acquiring large tracts of land, forming **haciendas** where Indigenous workers and eventually mestizos performed agriculture or ranching. Instead of direct tribute, laborers were paid minimal wages or bound by debt peonage. The hacienda system proved more sustainable for colonial elites, as it did not rely on the precarious encomienda grants, which the Crown could revoke. This shift continued into the 17th century, reshaping rural life and entrenching social inequalities for generations.

12.12 Enduring Legacies of the Early Colonial Period

By the late 16th century, New Spain was firmly established. A cathedral rose on the site of Tenochtitlán's Templo Mayor. Universities and printing presses appeared, fostering an educated class that blended European scholasticism with local realities. Indigenous communities, drastically reduced in population, nonetheless persisted, defending land titles and passing on traditions where possible.

This early colonial era laid the foundation for modern Mexico in several ways:

1. **Ethnic Diversity:** The mixing of Indigenous, European, and African peoples set the stage for a complex social hierarchy but also created a rich cultural heritage.
2. **Catholic Identity with Indigenous Roots:** The Church's pervasive presence influenced language, art, and community life, yet elements of pre-Hispanic religion and culture survived beneath the surface or merged into local Catholic practices.
3. **Economic Dependence on Silver and Agriculture:** Large-scale mining and hacienda agriculture directed the colony's wealth to Europe while transforming local landscapes.
4. **Institutional Frameworks:** Viceroys, audiencias, and cabildos structured governance, sometimes adapting to incorporate Indigenous leaders.

Although enormous suffering accompanied conquest—through diseases, forced labor, and cultural suppression—the resilience of Indigenous communities contributed to a uniquely blended society. This chapter closes with an understanding that "New Spain" was never purely Spanish, but an evolving mosaic of peoples, traditions, and negotiations.

CHAPTER 13

THE CHURCH AND SOCIETY IN COLONIAL MEXICO (16TH – 18TH CENTURIES)

In the centuries following the Spanish conquest, the Catholic Church became a powerful institution that touched every aspect of life in New Spain. From the very first friars who accompanied conquistadors, to the sprawling religious orders that built monasteries and influenced politics, the Church was both a spiritual guide and a formidable landowner. Its presence offered Indigenous communities new forms of education and charity, but also introduced an institution that could wield the Inquisition, regulate cultural expressions, and reinforce social hierarchies. This chapter explores the broad impact of the Church in colonial Mexico—its missionary origins, role in shaping morality and identity, economic power, and evolving relationship with royal authority as the colony approached the dawn of independence.

13.1 EARLY MISSIONARIES AND EVANGELIZATION

Franciscans, Dominicans, and Augustinians Arrive

Shortly after the fall of Tenochtitlán in 1521, Franciscan friars landed in central Mexico with the intention of converting Indigenous populations to Christianity. By learning local languages—most notably Nahuatl—they established common ground with communities still reeling from war, disease, and the collapse of the Aztec state. The **Dominicans** and **Augustinians** soon joined, and together these missionary orders founded **conventos** (missionary outposts and monastic houses).

- **Franciscan Doctrina**: The Franciscans instituted a form of religious instruction called *doctrina*, teaching basic prayers, the catechism, and Christian ethics. Indigenous children, especially from noble families, were encouraged to attend classes held in or near the newly built conventos.
- **Adaptation and Syncretism**: Despite official Church policy against "idolatry," many friars realized that outright destruction of indigenous rites would create resistance. As a result, they selectively incorporated local festivals, symbols, and traditions into Christian celebrations—a process that gave colonial Mexican Catholicism its unique syncretic flavor.

Defending Indigenous Rights (In Part)
Missionaries often witnessed the abuses of the **encomienda** system, in which Spanish encomenderos exerted heavy labor demands on Indigenous communities. Some clergy, notably **Bartolomé de las Casas**, wrote impassioned accounts condemning these injustices. While their advocacy did not end exploitation, it pressured the Crown to issue laws regulating encomenderos and led to new discussions about Indigenous welfare.

Expansion into Frontier Regions
Beyond central Mexico, friars ventured into regions such as Michoacán, Oaxaca, and later northward. Their goals included not only preaching but also establishing stable communities under Church guidance. In certain frontier zones, Franciscan and Dominican missions became de facto local governments, distributing farmland, teaching new agricultural techniques, and sometimes defending Indigenous converts from slavers or hostile Spanish colonists.

13.2 CHURCH STRUCTURE: DIOCESES, CLERGY, AND THE INQUISITION

Secular vs. Regular Clergy
To administer a growing flock, the Church in New Spain developed a two-tier system:

- **Regular clergy**: friars belonging to orders such as the Franciscans, Dominicans, Augustinians, and later the Jesuits. They lived communally under vows of poverty, chastity, and obedience. Regular clergy mostly staffed rural missions and conventos.
- **Secular clergy**: diocesan priests under the direct authority of bishops. They ran established parishes—often in towns and cities—and served under a hierarchical structure culminating in archbishops.

Over time, tensions surfaced when secular bishops sought to claim parishes originally founded by regular friars. Disputes might center on who would collect tithes, who governed local chapels, and how new expansions of Church presence would be organized.

Dioceses and the Archbishopric of Mexico
By royal and papal decrees, bishoprics formed in Puebla, Michoacán, Oaxaca, Guadalajara, and other key regions. Mexico City became an archbishopric, its

occupant holding authority over the other dioceses. This structure mirrored ecclesiastical setups in Spain. Through the system called the **Patronato Real**, the Spanish Crown heavily influenced the appointment of bishops, ensuring loyalty to royal policy.

The Holy Office of the Inquisition

Established to maintain Catholic orthodoxy, the **Inquisition** arrived in New Spain in the 1570s. Though it primarily targeted Spanish settlers suspected of heresy, blasphemy, or secret Jewish practices, it eventually extended scrutiny to anyone perceived as deviating from orthodox Catholicism. Indigenous converts were at first under missionary courts, but if they appeared to backslide into "idolatry," they could face Inquisition procedures. Punishments varied from public penance to fines, property confiscation, or, in extreme cases, imprisonment or death. Moreover, the Inquisition exercised censorship over books, limiting access to works deemed heretical or suspicious of Spanish authority.

Collecting Tithes and Building Wealth

The Church in New Spain collected the **tithe**—traditionally one-tenth of agricultural produce or its monetary equivalent. This revenue financed local parishes, clergy salaries, and church construction. Over time, wealthy orders and dioceses could invest in farmland, ranching, or provide loans to lay landowners. While some funds went to charitable works, critics accused the Church of amassing wealth that contradicted its spiritual mission.

13.3 MONASTERIES, JESUIT EDUCATION, AND SOCIAL INFLUENCE

Conventos as Cultural Hubs

Franciscans, Dominicans, and Augustinians erected large convento complexes in central Mexico, some with fortress-like exteriors and spacious courtyards. These conventos served multiple purposes:

1. **Evangelization Centers**: Hosting masses, confessions, and baptisms for Indigenous converts.
2. **Educational Outposts**: Teaching reading, writing, crafts, and rudimentary theology.
3. **Community Gathering Places**: Organizing festivities, distributing food aid during crises, and mediating disputes between local people and Spanish officials.

Jesuits Enter the Scene

Arriving in the mid-16th century, the **Jesuits** (Society of Jesus) focused strongly on education. They established **colegios** in major cities such as Mexico City and Puebla, offering advanced schooling in theology, philosophy, Latin grammar, and even mathematics. Some Jesuit colleges admitted Indigenous nobles or mestizos with means, thereby shaping an educated class loyal to Catholic orthodoxy.

- **Missions in the North**: The Jesuits also created mission settlements among nomadic or semi-nomadic peoples, teaching them agriculture and crafts. In regions like Sonora and Sinaloa, Jesuit missionaries endeavored to form stable communities, often facing resistance from settlers encroaching on Indigenous lands.

Hospitals and Charity

Religious orders founded hospitals in urban centers, treating those afflicted by European diseases and local ailments. Although treatment was limited by the era's medical knowledge, these institutions symbolized the Church's charitable reach. Monasteries and convents also coordinated almsgiving, distributed bread or maize in lean times, and supported orphans or the homeless. This benevolence boosted the Church's moral authority, even as it maintained close ties to the colonial power structure.

13.4 ENFORCING MORALITY AND SYNCRETIC RELIGION

Regulating Conduct

The Church oversaw a wide range of moral codes. Clergy preached against public drunkenness, sexual impropriety, or failure to attend mass. Reports of scandalous behavior—bigamy, "superstitions," or irreverent speech—could trigger Church-led investigations, though enforcement varied by region. Wealthy Spaniards or officials often found ways to escape serious punishments, while commoners might suffer harsh sentences for lesser transgressions.

Folk Catholicism and Local Festivals

For Indigenous communities, Catholic practice increasingly blended older cosmologies into saint cults, Marian devotions, and local celebrations. Dances formerly tied to harvest deities were repurposed for saints' feast days. Drums and wind instruments survived in religious processions, albeit dedicated to Christ or the Virgin Mary. Over generations, many devout Catholics in rural areas maintained partial knowledge of pre-Hispanic beliefs, integrating them seamlessly into daily worship.

13.5 THE CHURCH'S LANDHOLDING AND ECONOMIC POWER

Accumulating Estates and Mortgages

Thanks to donations from devout patrons and strategic purchases, certain monastic orders became substantial landowners. They ran haciendas producing wheat, sugar, or livestock, and used profits to fund new convents, build grand churches, or lend money to landowners at interest. This process granted the Church a vital role in rural economics.

- **Loans and Interest**: While the Church officially denounced usury, it often charged moderate interest rates on loans. Many lay landowners preferred dealing with ecclesiastical creditors, finding them more lenient in times of drought or poor harvest.

Conflict and Criticism

Secular authorities sometimes objected that the Church's acquisitions limited the Crown's taxable base. Philosophers and reformers criticized religious orders for living too luxuriously, contending that the vow of poverty clashed with expansive estates. Internal Church debates also flared: some members felt amassing property was a necessary means to sustain evangelization and charity, while others saw it as straying from spiritual ideals.

Cofradías and Community Support
Beyond large estates, Church-based confraternities (cofradías) thrived at the local level. These lay brotherhoods collected dues from members, paid for religious feasts, and provided mutual aid—such as funeral costs or help with medical expenses. They often operated smaller farmland plots or raised animals, generating income to host elaborate processions or sponsor local pilgrimages. Cofradías thus reinforced the Church's communal presence, blending devotion with practical support.

13.6 ART, ARCHITECTURE, AND SCHOLARSHIP

Cathedrals and Convento Styles
From the 16th to 18th centuries, Church-funded construction shaped the urban skyline. Early buildings bore Renaissance simplicity, but soon the flamboyant **Baroque** style rose to prominence, featuring ornate facades, gilded altarpieces, and swirling architectural details. Indigenous artisans trained by friars contributed carved stone details and wooden statues, subtly weaving local motifs (like eagle, jaguar, or floral patterns) into Christian iconography.

- **Puebla and Its Talavera Tiles**: In the city of Puebla, religious and civic buildings famously used Talavera ceramic tiles to decorate exteriors and interiors, reflecting a fusion of Spanish, Middle Eastern, and Indigenous influences.

Religious Painting and Sculpture
Religious orders patronized large workshops producing canvases of biblical scenes or saints, which adorned convent walls. Some paintings depicted New World landscapes or integrated local flora and fauna to give Christian stories a distinctive American flavor. Sculptors created polychrome statues for altars and processions, sometimes dressed in real fabric. These visual arts served as powerful teaching tools for a largely illiterate population, conveying narratives of salvation or moral lessons.

Monastic Libraries and Intellectual Pursuits
Friars who learned Indigenous languages compiled dictionaries, catechisms, and historical accounts. The most famous example is the **Florentine Codex** by

Bernardino de Sahagún, which documented Aztec culture from the perspective of both Indigenous informants and Spanish Catholic ideology. Monastic libraries stored volumes of theology, canon law, and local ethnographies. Later, Jesuit colleges advanced higher education, shaping an intellectual elite versed in Scholasticism yet increasingly aware of Enlightenment currents from Europe.

13.7 CHURCH PRIVILEGES, ROYAL REFORMS, AND THE LATE COLONIAL PERIOD

Ecclesiastical Immunities

Clergy in New Spain often enjoyed **fueros** (legal exemptions), meaning they faced ecclesiastical courts rather than civil ones. Bishops insisted on defending these privileges, seeing them as essential to the Church's autonomy. Secular officials, however, contended that priests or friars accused of secular crimes should not escape royal jurisdiction. Such disputes underscored the Church's semi-independent power within colonial society.

Bourbon Reforms

By the 18th century, Spain's Bourbon kings launched reforms to modernize colonial administration. These entailed reorganizing provinces into intendancies, reducing the wealth and influence of religious orders, and curtailing certain Church privileges in order to channel more revenue to the Crown. While some Church leaders complied, others resisted or negotiated partial agreements. The monarchy's attempt to centralize power and diminish clerical autonomy fostered tension among Church elites, wealthy criollos, and Indigenous communities who relied on ecclesiastical structures for representation.

Growing Discontent and the Road to Independence
As the colonial era neared its end, the Church remained deeply woven into daily life—teaching in village schools, hosting colorful festivals, and providing spiritual services. Yet a class of criollos—landowners, merchants, and some lower clergy—felt increasingly alienated by Spanish policy. Enlightenment ideas filtered into certain Church circles, sparking debates about reason, monarchy, and the moral justification of Spanish rule. Although many clergy remained loyal to the Crown, others would eventually support or at least sympathize with independence movements, believing that a new political framework might preserve Catholic faith while granting more autonomy to local communities.

CHAPTER 14

ECONOMIC FOUNDATIONS OF NEW SPAIN (16TH – 18TH CENTURIES)

While the Catholic Church shaped the spiritual and social landscape, the bedrock of colonial Mexico's material development lay in its economy. Silver mining, vast agricultural estates, and extensive trade networks bound New Spain to global markets across the Atlantic and Pacific. Indigenous communities provided much of the labor—often under oppressive conditions—while Spanish and criollo elites profited from the colony's natural resources. Over the centuries, these economic systems evolved through labor drafts, changing trade policies, and royal reforms, culminating in mounting tensions that would eventually feed independence movements.

14.1 THE RACE FOR GOLD AND THE DISCOVERY OF SILVER

Initial Gold Hopes
When Hernán Cortés and other conquistadors first arrived, they sought gold, believing Indigenous treasures hinted at limitless wealth. Initial plundering of Aztec hoards provided some precious metal, but the expected "mountains of gold" never materialized. The Spanish soon recognized that truly vast riches lay elsewhere.

Northern Silver Strikes
By the mid-16th century, explorers probing beyond the central valleys located rich silver veins in places such as **Zacatecas**, **Guanajuato**, and **San Luis Potosí**. This discovery transformed New Spain into one of the world's largest silver producers. The Crown imposed a **quinto real** (royal fifth) on mined silver, guaranteeing substantial revenue to fund Spain's European wars and imperial ventures. Mining towns sprouted rapidly, beckoning fortune seekers from all over the colony and from Spain itself.

Early Mining Challenges
Extracting silver was no simple task. Spaniards needed skilled laborers to dig tunnels and refine ore. Indigenous workers, already decimated by epidemic diseases, were forcibly recruited through the **encomienda** or special labor drafts.

Accidents, poor ventilation, and toxins took a severe toll on miners. Though wages could be marginally higher than in subsistence farming, the grueling conditions led to high turnover and persistent labor shortages.

14.2 LABOR SYSTEMS: ENCOMIENDA, REPARTIMIENTO, AND HACIENDAS

Encomienda and Transition to Repartimiento

Initially, many conquistadors received **encomiendas**—grants of Indigenous tribute and labor. Widespread abuses prompted royal decrees aiming to limit perpetual encomiendas. Over time, the Crown shifted to **repartimiento**, a rotational draft system where communities provided labor for mines or estates at minimal wages. Though regulated on paper, unscrupulous employers frequently exploited these workers, demanding extra days or paying in scrip valid only at company stores.

Haciendas and Debt Peonage

Beyond mining, Spanish settlers established **haciendas** for large-scale agriculture (wheat, sugar, livestock). Displaced from traditional communal lands, Indigenous peasants found themselves reliant on hacendados (estate owners). Many fell into **debt peonage**, where they borrowed money or goods and repaid the debt with labor—rarely escaping the cycle due to manipulative accounting.

- **Livestock Impact**: Sheep, cattle, and horses introduced by Spaniards also reshaped landscapes, often leading to overgrazing and competition over watering holes. Indigenous milpa systems faced displacement, intensifying rural poverty and dependency on colonial estates.

Social Stratification

While the **peninsulares** (Spaniards born in Europe) and some **criollos** (American-born Spaniards) grew wealthy through mining or haciendas, the majority of Indigenous and mestizo populations lived as laborers with few rights. Afro-descendant individuals, both free and enslaved, contributed to the workforce, particularly in sugar mills or livestock ranches. Racial and caste distinctions became entrenched, with the labor system reinforcing the colonial hierarchy.

14.3 MINING TOWNS AND THE "SILVER CIRCUIT"

Urban Development

Miners and entrepreneurs flocked to silver-rich sites, transforming them into bustling urban centers. In **Zacatecas**, for instance, the precarious hillside location did not deter rapid growth. By the 17th century, Zacatecas boasted churches, municipal buildings, and refined homes for the mine owners. Meanwhile, huddled shanties or small adobe dwellings lined the outskirts, housing Indigenous laborers, free Black workers, and mestizos.

- **Guanajuato**: Another leading silver producer, famed for mines like La Valenciana. Wealthy mine owners sponsored the construction of grand Baroque churches, lavish mansions, and civic festivals, even as miners endured harsh conditions underground.

Patio Process

An essential boost to productivity was the **patio process**, introduced around the 1550s. In large open-air courtyards, crushed ore was mixed with mercury, salt, and other reagents, forming an amalgam. By heating the amalgam, miners could evaporate the mercury and leave purified silver behind. Although revolutionary, this method exposed laborers to mercury fumes, causing neurological and physical harm. Nonetheless, the technique allowed Spanish authorities and private investors to extract huge amounts of silver more cheaply and quickly.

Transport and Security

Silver bullion or coins were transported on mule trains or in convoys to Mexico City and onward to Veracruz. Robbers, hostile Indigenous groups (resisting colonial encroachment), and rugged terrain made these routes perilous. The Crown sometimes provided armed escorts, understanding that safeguarding silver was paramount for sustaining Spanish imperial ambitions.

14.4 AGRICULTURE, LIVESTOCK, AND RURAL LIFE

Growth of Large Estates
Parallel to mining expansions, colonists established massive **haciendas** (estates) to cultivate wheat, sugarcane, or other cash crops, as well as raise cattle, sheep, and horses for both local consumption and export. Over time, certain families or religious orders accumulated multiple haciendas, transforming them into near self-sufficient domains with workshops, chapels, and living quarters for peons.

Debt Peonage and Village Life
A typical peon family lived in modest huts on estate land, receiving meager wages or rationed maize. When they needed extra money—for seeds, a wedding, or an emergency—they borrowed from the hacendado at interest. This debt, recorded in estate ledgers, prevented them from leaving until fully repaid. Generations thus remained bound to the same estate. Some peons supplemented their diets with small garden plots or raising poultry, but the estate's overarching control stifled upward mobility.

Environmental Transformations
Sheep and cattle ranching significantly altered Mexico's ecology. Large herds trampled grasslands, causing soil erosion. Traditional communal farmland, known as **calpulli** in many Indigenous towns, shrank in the face of Spanish enclosure. In some regions, local peoples adapted by herding goats or sheep themselves, but more often, they were pushed into marginal lands as Spaniards claimed prime pasture or water sources.

14.5 COMMERCIAL NETWORKS AND URBAN EXCHANGE

Mexico City as Commercial Hub
Rebuilt over the Aztec capital, Mexico City soon overshadowed all other towns in New Spain. Mule caravans from the silver mines and cargo wagons from the Gulf Coast converged there, making it the prime market for raw materials and European imports. Merchant guilds, known as **consulados**, oversaw pricing and quality control, ensuring goods like wine, olive oil, or fabrics from Spain were distributed throughout the colony.

Provincial Towns and Fairs
While Mexico City dominated, secondary cities—Puebla, Querétaro, Guadalajara, Valladolid (Morelia)—linked regional producers to larger markets. Periodic fairs,

such as those in Jalapa (Xalapa) near Veracruz, brought merchants together for major trading events. Landowners, mine representatives, and shopkeepers negotiated deals, bartered or sold at fixed prices, and formed alliances that spanned large distances.

- **Puebla's Artisan Culture**: Known for Talavera ceramics, Puebla became a manufacturing center that supplied decorative tiles and household pottery to parishes, conventos, and private homes across New Spain.

Local Markets and Artisan Economies
In smaller towns, weekly markets served rural populations. Indigenous women sold tortillas, chilies, beans, or handwoven textiles. Mestizo craftsmen might offer iron tools, leather goods, or simple furniture. This grassroots commerce allowed for cultural interactions and modest social mobility, even though the broader economic structure was controlled by Spanish policies and large estate owners.

14.6 ATLANTIC AND PACIFIC TRADE ROUTES

The Flota System
Keen to protect its American trade against pirates and rival European powers, Spain enforced the **flota** (fleet) system. Galleons sailed in convoy between Veracruz and Seville (later Cádiz), guarded by military vessels. Officially, all transatlantic trade had to pass through these fleets. As a result, cargo holds were crammed with silver ingots, cochineal (a valuable red dye from insects), and other colonial goods. In return, New Spain received European textiles, metal goods, and wines.

- **Smuggling**: Heavy taxes and bureaucratic delays encouraged illicit trade. Dutch, English, and French ships frequented remote coves to barter contraband goods, and local officials often turned a blind eye in exchange for bribes.

The Manila Galleon
A defining feature of New Spain's economy was the **Manila Galleon** route, linking Acapulco with Manila in the Philippines. This trade corridor allowed Spanish merchants to exchange silver for Chinese silks, porcelains, and spices, which then circulated within the colony or traveled on to Europe. Though only a few

galleons sailed each year, the profits could be staggering. Asian goods influenced Mexican art, clothing, and cuisine, creating a unique cultural fusion. However, storms, pirates, and the inherent risk of long Pacific voyages sometimes led to catastrophic losses.

Strategic Importance of Acapulco and Veracruz

- **Acapulco**: Served as the Manila Galleon's Pacific port. During trade fairs, the city teemed with buyers, from humble peddlers to wealthy criollo families.
- **Veracruz**: The main Gulf port for transatlantic fleets, handling silver exports, returning European imports, and occasionally enslaved Africans. Harsh tropical diseases plagued travelers, making Veracruz notorious for fevers.

14.7 ROYAL REVENUES, TAXATION, AND CORRUPTION

The Crown's Financial Gains
Spain collected substantial wealth from New Spain via:

1. **The Quinto Real**: a 20% cut of all precious metals mined.
2. **Alcabala (Sales Tax)**: imposed on goods sold in markets.

3. **Tribute**: demanded from Indigenous towns, often paid in maize, cotton, or local crafts.
4. **Customs Duties**: on goods entering or leaving ports.

These taxes funded royal expenses in Europe, fueling Spain's military campaigns and courtly extravagances. Nonetheless, corruption among colonial officials—skimming profits, forging records, or ignoring contraband shipments—eroded what the Crown could effectively collect.

Bourbon Reforms
By the 18th century, the **Bourbon** dynasty in Spain recognized the need for tighter control. New administrative units, called **intendancies**, tried to streamline tax collection and reduce local corruption. The Crown also championed the modernization of mining, offering incentives for improved technology and better refining processes. While these reforms increased revenue somewhat, they alienated local elites who disliked the monarchy's intrusion into their affairs.

Criollo Resentments
A growing class of **criollos**—American-born people of Spanish descent—controlled substantial land and commercial ventures. They felt overshadowed by peninsular Spaniards occupying high offices and resented taxes flowing out to Europe. Enlightenment ideas questioning absolute monarchy and endorsing economic liberalism emboldened some criollos to envision self-governance free from stifling Spanish oversight.

14.8 DAILY LIFE FOR LABORERS AND ARTISANS

Miners at Risk
Mining towns like Zacatecas, Guanajuato, and Real del Monte attracted laborers seeking better wages than subsistence farming offered. They worked in deep shafts, hauling ore, or on **patios** with toxic mercury. While some managed to save money or set up small side businesses, many fell victim to accidents or illness, leading to high turnover and a constant need for new recruits.

Hacienda Peons and Indigenous Communities
In the countryside, Indigenous families tried to maintain their own milpa plots alongside estate duties. Some older communal structures survived, but land

fragmentation forced many to rely on wage labor or precarious sharecropping. Although conditions were harsh, local markets offered occasional respite—people exchanged surplus produce for clothing or metal tools, forging small pockets of autonomy within a larger oppressive system.

Crafts and Local Markets

Artisans produced footwear, simple textiles, saddlery, and pottery for sale in weekly or monthly markets. For many rural mestizos and Indigenous people, these markets were vital social and economic gatherings, enabling them to earn extra money and keep in touch with broader developments. Over time, specialized localities became known for particular crafts, and certain families built modest fortunes as recognized artisans.

14.9 TOWARD INDEPENDENCE: ECONOMIC FACTORS AND SOCIAL PRESSURES

Seeds of Discontent

By the late 18th century, multiple strains tested the colonial economic framework:

1. **Heavy Tax Burdens**: The Crown's fiscal demands weighed on merchants, miners, and farmers alike.
2. **Rigid Mercantilism**: Official trade monopolies and shipping restrictions strangled entrepreneurial freedom, fueling a black market.
3. **Labor Exploitation**: Forced drafts in mines, continued land losses, and mounting debt peonage stifled Indigenous and mestizo prospects.

Enlightenment Ideas and Criollo Aspirations

Wealthy criollos engaged with Enlightenment treatises—some imported clandestinely—proposing individual rights, property freedoms, and local governance. While not all advocated outright separation from Spain, they questioned the monarchy's paternalistic rule and the privileges peninsular Spaniards enjoyed. Meanwhile, long-suffering Indigenous communities had their own histories of rebellion, albeit scattered and localized, responding to land dispossession or tribute hikes.

Bourbon Reforms as a Catalyst

The Bourbon Reforms accelerated these tensions. While introduced to streamline finances, the reforms curtailed certain local autonomies and threatened entrenched interests. The monarchy's push to wrest more profit from the colony, combined with an emerging sense of regional identity, laid a powder keg of discontent. The Napoleonic invasion of Spain in 1808, which disrupted the Crown's authority, would finally ignite this tinder, leading to independence movements that harnessed both economic and social grievances.

14.10 LEGACY OF THE COLONIAL ECONOMY

By the early 19th century, New Spain's economy had generated immense wealth for the Spanish Crown and for certain colonial elites. Silver from Mexican mines helped finance European warfare, while the Manila Galleon made the colony a global crossroads linking Asia, the Americas, and Europe. Agricultural estates, though often exploitative, supplied staple crops and introduced new livestock-based economies. Yet these developments rested on fragile foundations of forced labor, social stratification, and restricted trade policies.

Ultimately, economic grievances intertwined with political and ideological ferment. As cries for autonomy grew louder, the harsh realities faced by miners, hacienda peons, and Indigenous communities weighed heavily on the conscience of emerging criollo leaders. The complex web of mercantilist rules, heavy taxes, and Bourbon centralization pushed New Spain toward a watershed moment. When independence finally arrived, it would transform not only political governance but also the entrenched economic structures that had defined Mexico for three centuries under Spanish rule.

CHAPTER 15

ENLIGHTENMENT AND REFORM (LATE 18TH CENTURY – EARLY 19TH CENTURY)

Throughout the 18th century, New Spain underwent significant cultural and intellectual changes, in part due to the **Bourbon Reforms** introduced by Spanish monarchs. These reforms sought to modernize the empire's administration and increase royal revenue, but they also opened the door to new ideas from Europe. The **Enlightenment**, with its emphasis on reason, science, and the questioning of traditional authority, gradually influenced some colonial elites—especially **criollos** (American-born Spaniards), who felt limited by Spanish policies. Beneath the surface, a growing dissatisfaction with royal control, economic restrictions, and social inequalities laid the groundwork for deeper calls for reform. This chapter explores how Enlightenment thought entered New Spain, how local intellectuals reacted, and how Bourbon Reforms shaped governance, culminating in tensions that would soon spur the movement toward independence.

15.1 THE CONTEXT OF THE BOURBON REFORMS

The Bourbon Monarchy in Spain

In 1700, the Spanish throne passed to the **Bourbon** dynasty, originally from France. Over time, these new monarchs introduced a series of administrative and economic measures—collectively known as the Bourbon Reforms—aimed at centralizing power and modernizing the empire's vast territories. For New Spain, this meant:

- **Reorganizing provinces** into **intendancies** led by officials loyal to the Crown, bypassing local elites who had enjoyed considerable autonomy.
- **Revamping tax collection**, cracking down on contraband, and strengthening monopolies over certain goods like tobacco.
- **Streamlining the military** by establishing local militias, ensuring the colony could defend itself from foreign threats without relying solely on Spain's distant resources.

Impact on Local Elites

These reforms delivered mixed results. On the one hand, improved administration and the push for economic efficiency could benefit trade and mining output. On the other hand, many **criollos**—especially powerful landowners, merchants, and intellectuals—resented losing local privileges. They chafed under new taxes and the appointment of more **peninsulares** (Spaniards born in Europe) to high posts, a shift that seemed to sideline American-born Spaniards despite their equal or greater wealth.

Cultural Changes and the Spread of Secular Ideas

Alongside administrative overhauls, the Crown encouraged secularization in education. Where the Church had once dominated schooling, the monarchy started promoting royal colleges and scientific academies. While Catholic doctrine remained primary, more worldly subjects—natural sciences, mathematics, modern languages—found a place in curricula. Slowly, the realm of learning expanded beyond strictly religious confines.

15.2 THE RISE OF ENLIGHTENMENT IDEAS IN NEW SPAIN

Intellectual Currents from Europe

Beginning in the mid-18th century, treatises by Enlightenment writers like **Voltaire**, **Montesquieu**, and **Rousseau** began circulating in New Spain, often in heavily censored or clandestine forms. Their core messages—skepticism of absolute monarchy, promotion of reason and scientific inquiry, and calls for personal liberty—found a receptive audience among certain criollo and mestizo intellectuals.

- **Censorship and the Inquisition**: Strict oversight remained, and many works arrived surreptitiously via smuggling or travelers returning from Europe. The Holy Office of the Inquisition continued to ban texts seen as heretical or politically dangerous, but this only heightened their allure for curious minds.

Salons and Literary Societies

Some urban centers, notably Mexico City and Puebla, hosted informal gatherings—much like European **salons**—where educated men (and occasionally women) discussed new scientific discoveries, essays on governance, or critiques of scholastic tradition. **Literary societies** or academies formed, sometimes with royal backing, to study botany, physics, or local history. These associations nurtured a budding generation of Mexican-born scholars who valued empirical observation over inherited dogma.

Role of the Jesuits
Before their expulsion in 1767, the **Jesuits** often led the way in rigorous scholarship. They operated some of the colony's finest colleges, teaching advanced mathematics, astronomy, and classical languages. Certain Jesuit intellectuals embraced Enlightenment principles, fusing them with Catholic theology. After their expulsion—part of a Bourbon effort to reduce Church influence—Jesuit scholars carried their ideas elsewhere, but the seeds they planted in New Spain persisted.

15.3 BOURBON REFORMS IN PRACTICE: ADMINISTRATION AND ECONOMY

Reorganized Provinces and Intendancies
To tighten royal oversight, Spain subdivided New Spain into **intendancies** headed by **intendants**—bureaucrats chosen for their loyalty rather than local ties. These officials were tasked with boosting tax revenues, modernizing local infrastructures, and checking corruption. In places like Guanajuato (famous for silver mines) or Valladolid (Morelia), intendants sought to optimize mining practices, road maintenance, and the collection of tributes from Indigenous communities.

- **Opposition and Tensions**: Local cabildos (municipal councils) or provincial elites often resisted these changes, fearing the intrusion on their longstanding privileges. Conflicts arose when intendants clashed with entrenched families who had managed local affairs for generations.

Military and Militia Reforms
Spain's losses in European conflicts underscored the need for colonial militias. The Bourbon monarchy encouraged the formation of locally recruited regiments—often led by criollo officers—who were expected to defend against foreign invasions. While this gave some criollos a taste of military command, it also underscored the Crown's strategy of controlling them via structured hierarchies.

- **Increased Criollo Consciousness**: Serving as militia officers fostered a sense of identity among American-born Spaniards, who recognized they played a pivotal role in defending the colony. This sometimes led them to question why peninsulares dominated higher echelons of civil and ecclesiastical offices.

Economic Liberalization and Monopolies
The Crown partially relaxed certain trade barriers, allowing limited commerce with other Spanish colonies and expanding lawful ports. Nonetheless, key products—tobacco, gunpowder, salt—remained under royal monopolies that generated substantial revenue but frustrated local producers. The monarchy's desire to "open up" the economy while still preserving revenue streams created a contradictory environment that offered glimpses of freer trade but fell short of genuine economic liberalism.

15.4 CHANGING VIEWS ON EDUCATION, SCIENCE, AND THE CHURCH

Secular Schools and Scientific Clubs
While Catholic institutions still dominated formal education, a few secular schools or scientific clubs emerged in the major cities, teaching Enlightenment

methods of observation and experimentation. Subjects like natural history, botany, and mineralogy were especially appealing, given New Spain's rich flora and valuable mineral deposits.

- **Notable Figures**: Individuals like **José Antonio de Alzate y Ramírez**, a Mexican polymath, published scientific journals examining local fauna, celestial phenomena, and engineering challenges. His efforts showcased a distinctly American viewpoint, challenging purely Eurocentric scholarship.

Clerical Participation in Enlightenment
Despite the monarchy's bid to reduce ecclesiastical power, many priests, especially younger ones, embraced new learning. Their sermons sometimes blended calls for moral reawakening with subtle critiques of corruption—both in Church ranks and civil institutions. Yet the overarching Church structure, wary of losing authority, remained ambivalent about Enlightenment ideals. Some bishops welcomed moderate reforms, while others denounced them as breeding heresy or disrespect for tradition.

Challenges to Inquisitorial Censorship
Enlightened clergy and criollo laymen increasingly questioned the Inquisition's heavy-handed suppression of literature. As Bourbon officials themselves championed a more "enlightened" monarchy, the Holy Office found it trickier to justify banning works on purely philosophical or scientific grounds. Still, suspicion lingered: too close an embrace of Enlightenment values risked accusations of heresy. Writers walked a delicate line, couching critiques of monarchy or clerical authority in careful language.

15.5 SOCIAL AND CULTURAL CONSEQUENCES

Growing Criollo Self-Awareness
For decades, criollos had compared themselves unfavorably to peninsulares, who monopolized top colonial positions. Now, with Enlightenment concepts of equality, merit, and national wealth, many American-born Spaniards began asking: why should mother Spain reap the colony's silver if local men possessed the expertise? Why should the best offices go to outsiders, ignoring criollo loyalty and competence? Such sentiments subtly eroded the monarchy's legitimacy.

Literary and Artistic Flourishing
Influenced by Enlightenment tastes, literature in New Spain began shifting from purely religious or Baroque styles to more secular, neoclassical themes. Poets and essayists praised reason and civic virtue, exploring the idea of a distinct Mexican identity. Artists took inspiration from European neoclassicism while weaving in local motifs—leading to new hybrid art forms that departed from earlier, heavily religious aesthetics.

Ethnic and Caste Dynamics
While Enlightenment ideals talked of human equality, colonial society remained locked into the caste system. Most Indigenous peoples, mestizos, and Afro-descendant populations still faced discrimination, forced labor, or limited social mobility. A small fraction of mestizos found educational opportunities in new secular schools or militia roles, forging alliances with upwardly mobile criollos. But for the majority, Enlightenment rhetoric had little practical impact unless it translated into tangible reforms on labor, tribute, and representation.

15.6 OPPOSITION, UNEASE, AND THE PATH TOWARD REFORM

Resistance from Traditionalists
Some high-ranking clergy and conservative Spaniards viewed Enlightenment ideas with alarm. They feared that emphasizing reason, personal freedoms, and "modern" governance would undermine the divine-right monarchy and Church authority. Preachers sometimes railed against "French" philosophies, blaming them for moral decay or rebellious notions.

Failed Attempts at Broader Reform
Despite glimpses of progress, the Bourbon Reforms fell short for many criollos who hoped for deeper commercial freedoms and recognized meritocracy. Administrative changes often ended up reinforcing monarchy-driven revenue extraction. The continuing ban on free trade with foreign nations, as well as heavy restrictions on local industries, convinced many that the Crown would never allow genuine equality for New Spain.

Economic Tensions and Unrest
A series of local riots and small-scale rebellions flared up in the late 18th century, some sparked by new taxes or forced labor demands. In New Spain, the most famous case was the 1780s "Revolt of the Machetes" in the outskirts of Mexico

City—albeit minor, it signaled growing resentment among rural commoners. Meanwhile, silver exports soared, and wealthy mine owners or merchants thrived. The dichotomy between prosperity for a few and hardship for the many fed latent anger.

15.7 THE LEGACY OF ENLIGHTENMENT AND REFORM

By the turn of the 19th century, Enlightenment ideas had found a foothold in New Spain's intellectual circles. The Bourbon Reforms, while successful in some aspects (like improved revenue and partial administrative modernization), ultimately alienated large segments of colonial society—particularly the rising criollo class who sought a more open economy and political influence commensurate with their wealth and local roots. Even some liberal-minded clergy and officials believed that monarchy's paternalistic grip held back New Spain's potential.

The stage was thus set for a dramatic shift. When Spain itself was plunged into crisis—courtesy of the Napoleonic Wars—criollo leaders saw an opportunity to demand changes or even full autonomy. Inspired by Enlightenment principles and fed up with the colonial system's contradictions, they would soon launch a struggle that would transform New Spain into an independent nation. The story of that struggle unfolds in the next chapter.

CHAPTER 16

THE INDEPENDENCE MOVEMENT (1808 – 1821)

By the dawn of the 19th century, discontent simmered throughout New Spain. Enlightenment ideals had emboldened **criollos** to envision a society where American-born citizens held greater power, while heavy taxation, forced labor drafts, and strict trade regulations alienated Indigenous communities and mestizos. The immediate catalyst, however, came from abroad. When Napoleon invaded Spain in 1808, deposing King Ferdinand VII, the colonial administration in Mexico City faced a legitimacy crisis. Rival governing bodies emerged, and revolutionary conspiracies took shape. This chapter examines how local grievances coalesced into a movement for independence, starting with the call of **Father Miguel Hidalgo** and culminating in the triumph of a new, if fragile, Mexican state.

16.1 INTERNATIONAL CRISIS AND LOCAL REACTIONS

Napoleon's Invasion of Spain

In 1808, Napoleon forced the Spanish king, Ferdinand VII, to abdicate in favor of Napoleon's brother, Joseph Bonaparte. Many Spaniards and colonials refused to recognize Joseph as legitimate, pledging loyalty to the deposed Ferdinand. But with the monarchy effectively absent, questions arose: who governed New Spain now? Should loyalty remain with the old Crown, or could local authorities form their own governing juntas?

Competing Governing Factions

- **Peninsular Loyalists**: High-ranking officials and conservative Spaniards insisted that the viceroy rule in Ferdinand's name until he reclaimed the throne.
- **Criollo Reformers**: Some elites argued that, in the king's absence, sovereignty reverted to the people of New Spain, who could form a local junta or congress. They did not necessarily seek complete separation from Spain at first; they wanted autonomy and local governance reforms.
- **Radical Conspiracies**: Small circles of intellectuals in cities like Querétaro and Valladolid (Morelia) began contemplating outright independence,

inspired by the successes of the American Revolution (1776) and the early phases of revolution in France.

Economic Hardships

As warfare disrupted transatlantic trade, silver exports declined, and the Crown demanded even higher taxes to finance European conflicts. Indigenous communities, already overburdened, faced new tribute hikes. Many saw the peninsular bureaucracy as incompetent or corrupt, fueling local anger. Meanwhile, criollo landowners and merchants believed their wealth was being squandered to prop up a distant monarchy.

16.2 THE CONSPIRACY OF QUERÉTARO AND HIDALGO'S CALL

Secret Gatherings in Querétaro

By 1809 and 1810, a clandestine group of criollos and sympathetic clergy met in Querétaro to discuss the future. Led by **Josefa Ortiz de Domínguez** (La Corregidora) and her husband Miguel Domínguez, along with military officers like **Ignacio Allende**, they formulated plans to declare a local junta in the name of Ferdinand VII or possibly to break away entirely. Among their confederates was **Father Miguel Hidalgo y Costilla**, a parish priest in Dolores known for liberal ideas and sympathy toward Indigenous parishioners.

Uncovering the Plot

Spanish officials grew suspicious of irregular gatherings, and in September 1810, they uncovered the conspirators' plans earlier than the group anticipated. Realizing they had to act swiftly, Allende rushed to warn Hidalgo that arrests were imminent. Rather than flee, Hidalgo decided to seize the moment.

El Grito de Dolores (16 September 1810)

On the morning of **September 16**, in the town of Dolores (present-day Dolores Hidalgo, Guanajuato), Father Hidalgo rang his church bell and issued what became known as the **Grito de Dolores**—a cry calling parishioners to rise against Spanish oppression. He invoked loyalty to the Virgin of Guadalupe, symbolically uniting Catholic devotion with the struggle for justice. His words rallied a massive, mostly rural crowd—Indigenous villagers, mestizos, and a sprinkling of criollos. Thus began the first major insurgent movement in colonial Mexico.

16.3 EARLY INSURGENCY: HIDALGO AND ALLENDE

March to Guanajuato
Hidalgo's rapidly assembled army, armed with farm tools, slings, and a few muskets, headed toward Guanajuato—an important mining city with a significant Spanish population. In late September 1810, insurgents besieged the city's fortress-like **Alhóndiga de Granaditas**, where panicked Spaniards and loyalists had taken refuge. After fierce fighting, the insurgents seized the building. Chaos followed, with looting and violence that unnerved even Hidalgo's supporters.

Debates Within the Insurgent Ranks
While Hidalgo wanted sweeping social changes—proposing an end to tribute and the caste system—some criollo officers worried about unchecked violence against Spaniards and peninsulares. They feared the revolt might devolve into class warfare. **Ignacio Allende**, a more conservative military officer, clashed with Hidalgo's approach. Nonetheless, the insurgent army grew, attracting those seeking relief from oppression, as well as opportunists lured by rumors of Spanish wealth.

16.4 EARLY VICTORIES AND RETREATS

Rapid Expansion and Hesitation
Emboldened by their success in Guanajuato, Hidalgo's forces advanced toward Mexico City. Along the way, they captured Valladolid (Morelia) and other towns with minimal resistance, as local populations joined or acquiesced. But at the threshold of the capital, Hidalgo hesitated. The Spanish defenses in Mexico City were strong, and rumors of professional troops arrived to protect the viceroy. Some historians argue that seizing the city swiftly might have ended colonial rule prematurely, but Hidalgo doubted his untrained peasant army could hold it.

Calderón Bridge Defeat
Regrouping near Guadalajara, Hidalgo tried to consolidate his territorial gains. Yet, the royalist forces—bolstered by peninsular loyalists and better-equipped soldiers—counterattacked. In January 1811, at the **Battle of the Calderón Bridge**, the insurgent army suffered a decisive defeat. Lacking cohesion and modern weaponry, Hidalgo's forces scattered. Allende, upset by Hidalgo's leadership style, assumed more control, but the insurgency's momentum had waned.

Capture and Execution of Hidalgo
Retreating north, Hidalgo, Allende, and other leaders hoped to reorganize. However, in March 1811, they were betrayed and captured near Monclova by royalist troops. Spanish authorities tried Hidalgo for treason and heresy, defrocked him, and executed him on July 30, 1811. His death, though a blow to morale, transformed him into a martyr for the independence cause. Meanwhile, leadership shifted to other figures, including **José María Morelos y Pavón**, who would revitalize the insurgency.

16.5 MORELOS AND THE SECOND PHASE OF THE REBELLION

José María Morelos y Pavón
A former student of Hidalgo's, **Morelos** was a parish priest of mixed Indigenous and African descent. After Hidalgo's capture, he took up the banner of rebellion in southern Mexico. Unlike Hidalgo, Morelos was an adept strategist who organized smaller, disciplined forces. He aimed to liberate the southern provinces and create a stable revolutionary government.

Military Campaigns in the South
Between 1811 and 1813, Morelos's troops achieved notable successes in regions like Michoacán, Oaxaca, and parts of the Pacific coast. They disrupted royalist supply lines and established insurgent strongholds. Despite limited resources, they effectively used guerrilla tactics. Morelos also cultivated alliances with some local Indigenous communities by promising the end of tribute and better protection of their lands.

The Congress of Chilpancingo (1813)
In Chilpancingo, Morelos convened a **congress** of insurgent leaders, aiming to formalize the independence movement. Here, they drafted the **"Sentimientos de la Nación"** (Sentiments of the Nation), which declared:

1. Independence from Spain.
2. Catholicism as the sole religion (reflecting the insurgents' desire to maintain religious unity).
3. Elimination of the caste system, tribute, and slavery.
4. Establishment of popular sovereignty, with principles akin to Enlightenment doctrines of representative governance.

Though symbolic, this assembly represented a crucial step toward forging a new national identity.

16.6 SPANISH COUNTEROFFENSIVE AND THE EXECUTION OF MORELOS

Royalist Resistance
Alarmed by the insurgency's organization, Viceroy Félix María Calleja mounted a harsh counteroffensive. Royalist armies recaptured key cities, forcing Morelos and his congress to move frequently. Volunteers for the insurgents remained plentiful in rural areas, yet the lack of heavy artillery and steady supplies limited their ability to hold larger towns indefinitely.

Capture and Execution of Morelos
In late 1815, after several setbacks, Morelos was captured by royalist forces. Like Hidalgo, he faced a trial for treason and was defrocked before execution. His death momentarily fractured the insurgency's leadership, casting the movement

into a more dispersed guerrilla phase. Still, Morelos's legislative and military innovations laid groundwork that persisted, influencing later rebels.

Guerrilla Warfare and Regional Leaders
From 1816 onward, the rebellion became more fragmented. Fighters like **Vicente Guerrero**, **Guadalupe Victoria**, and others led local pockets of resistance. They executed hit-and-run raids, controlling parts of the countryside where royalist presence was weak. The monarchy poured resources into stamping out these cells, but the mountainous terrain and local support allowed insurgents to survive.

16.7 FROM STALEMATE TO OPPORTUNITY: FACTORS LEADING TO FINAL VICTORY

Monarchical Shifts in Spain
By 1820, Spain itself faced political turmoil. A liberal revolt forced King Ferdinand VII to restore the **Constitution of Cádiz** (originally drafted in 1812 but previously suppressed), effectively limiting royal power. Spanish conservatives, alarmed by liberal ascendancy, saw the transatlantic colonies as potential strongholds of traditional monarchy. Meanwhile, in Mexico, a new dynamic emerged.

The Plan of Iguala and Iturbide's Role

A royalist officer turned opportunist, **Agustín de Iturbide**, recognized that continued warfare drained resources. He brokered secret contacts with insurgent leaders, including Vicente Guerrero. Together, they issued the **Plan of Iguala** (February 24, 1821), proclaiming:

1. **Independence** from Spain under a constitutional monarchy.
2. **Unity** among peninsulares and criollos—ending caste rivalries at least in principle.
3. **Roman Catholic monopoly** on religion.

This plan appealed to both conservative landowners who feared social upheaval and insurgents desperate for a final settlement. It also assured Spaniards that their property and positions would be respected if they supported the new arrangement.

Treaty of Córdoba

As royal control crumbled, the last viceroy of New Spain reluctantly negotiated with Iturbide, resulting in the **Treaty of Córdoba** (August 1821), which recognized Mexico's independence under the terms of the Plan of Iguala. This momentous event ended three centuries of Spanish colonial rule. The victorious army, known as the **Ejército Trigarante** (Army of the Three Guarantees: Religion, Independence, and Unity), triumphantly entered Mexico City in late September 1821, sealing Mexico's birth as a sovereign state.

16.8 LEGACIES AND CHALLENGES OF THE INDEPENDENCE STRUGGLE

Diverse Motivations and Outcomes

The independence movement united a broad coalition—criollo elites resentful of Spanish centralism, liberal clergy inspired by Enlightenment ideals, and Indigenous or mestizo fighters yearning for an end to tributes and oppression. However, once Spain's power collapsed, deep divisions reemerged. Elite criollos often aimed to preserve social order, while popular classes wanted radical reforms that the new government might not deliver.

Figures of Independence

- **Hidalgo and Morelos**: Revered as martyrs and fathers of the insurgency, they symbolized the possibility of a fairer society.
- **Iturbide**: Though crucial in sealing independence, he later declared himself Emperor Agustín I, a move that alienated liberals. His short-lived empire fell by 1823.

Social and Economic Turmoil

Years of war devastated the colony's economy. Mines were abandoned, agricultural production plummeted, and widespread chaos impeded trade. The new government faced the daunting task of rebuilding infrastructure while forging a stable political framework. Meanwhile, the Church, still influential, negotiated its place in the post-independence order, seeking to preserve privileges while adapting to a secularizing environment.

Seeds of Future Conflicts

The independence victory did not immediately resolve issues of caste discrimination, land rights, or the balance between central authority and regional autonomy. Many Indigenous communities found that the new nation's criollo leaders were less than eager to fulfill promises of land restitution or equality. Nonetheless, the establishment of Mexico as an independent state opened a new chapter in which these questions could, at least in theory, be addressed by Mexicans themselves rather than foreign rulers.

16.9 CONCLUSION: MEXICO ON THE THRESHOLD OF A NEW ERA

From the moment Father Hidalgo rang the bell in Dolores to the entrance of the Ejercito Trigarante in Mexico City, the independence struggle spanned over a decade of shifting alliances, brutal battles, and ideological evolution. At its core, it was a conflict propelled by Enlightenment ideals, local grievances, economic hardship, and the destabilization of Spain's monarchy.

With independence achieved in 1821, Mexico entered an era of intense experimentation—monarchy or republic, centralism or federalism, conservative or liberal governance—seeking to define its own identity and address the legacies of colonialism. The immediate future would be fraught with internal power struggles, foreign interventions, and debates over the role of the Church and the shape of the new nation. Yet, the passion and sacrifice of insurgents like Hidalgo, Morelos, Guerrero, and countless anonymous fighters ensured that the people of Mexico would, from that point on, steer their own destiny.

CHAPTER 17

THE EARLY REPUBLIC (1821 – MID-19TH CENTURY)

After achieving independence from Spain in 1821, Mexico entered a turbulent period characterized by competing visions of governance, struggles over central versus regional power, economic instability, and the search for a unifying national identity. The nation initially experimented with a short-lived monarchy under **Agustín de Iturbide**, but soon transitioned to a republic. This new republic, however, was rife with political rivalries, foreign debts, and social divisions. Amidst repeated coups, financial crises, and attempts to define a functional constitution, leaders like **Guadalupe Victoria**, **Antonio López de Santa Anna**, and numerous regional caudillos (strongmen) vied for influence. This chapter explores how Mexico's early republic formed, the major conflicts that shaped it, and the enduring consequences for the young nation's political culture.

17.1 THE MEXICAN EMPIRE OF ITURBIDE

Plan of Iguala and the First Empire
The **Plan of Iguala** (1821) and the subsequent **Treaty of Córdoba** ended Spanish colonial rule but envisioned a constitutional monarchy. Agustín de Iturbide—once a royalist officer turned independence champion—was crowned **Emperor Agustín I** in mid-1822, hoping to stabilize the new state. Many had supported Iturbide as a unifying figure who could balance liberal and conservative factions.

Criticism and Downfall
Despite the pomp, Iturbide's reign quickly drew criticism. Liberal politicians, especially in regions outside Mexico City, accused him of centralizing power and stifling the fledgling congress. Economic woes persisted; Spain refused to recognize Mexican independence, hampering trade. When Iturbide dissolved the congress in late 1822, opposition crystallized. By March 1823, facing widespread unrest and the **Plan of Casa Mata** (which demanded restoration of a republican congress), Iturbide abdicated and went into exile. He returned in 1824, only to be arrested and executed—his brief empire consigned to history.

Republican Ideals Take Hold

With the emperor gone, the path to a republic opened. A constituent congress convened, declaring Mexico a federal republic in late 1823. This shift reflected Enlightenment-influenced liberal thought, emphasizing representative institutions and checks on executive power. Yet Mexico still had to figure out how to implement these ideals in a vast, diverse territory scarred by the independence wars.

17.2 EARLY FEDERAL EXPERIMENTS AND CONSTITUTIONS

Constitution of 1824

In October 1824, congress approved a constitution inspired by the U.S. and Spanish liberal constitutions. It established Mexico as a **federal republic**, dividing powers among executive, legislative, and judicial branches. Each state received autonomy, electing its own governor and legislature. Catholicism was retained as the official religion, reflecting the Church's continuing influence.

Guadalupe Victoria's Presidency

Guadalupe Victoria became the republic's first president (1824–1829). An independence hero, he aimed to calm factional disputes. However, the new government faced multiple challenges:

- **Financial Crises**: War had left Mexico with heavy debts and a ruined economy, forcing the government to borrow from British creditors.
- **Internal Revolts**: Regional caudillos, unhappy with limited resources or suspecting centralist meddling, rose in rebellion.
- **Foreign Pressures**: Spain threatened reconquest, and European powers watched warily, questioning Mexico's stability and creditworthiness.

Ideological Splits: Federalists vs. Centralists

A major divide soon appeared between **Federalists** and **Centralists**:

- **Federalists** favored strong state autonomy, minimal central control, and progressive reforms, such as loosening Church privileges.
- **Centralists** believed a powerful national government was necessary to unify Mexico, often aligning with conservative ideals that supported traditional institutions like the military and clergy.

This rivalry fueled cyclical coups and amendments to the constitution, with each faction seizing power through alliances with ambitious generals.

17.3 SANTA ANNA'S RISE AND SHIFTING ALLIANCES

Antonio López de Santa Anna

A charismatic yet mercurial figure, **Santa Anna** epitomized the early republic's instability. He initially supported Iturbide, then opposed him, championed federalism before pivoting to centralism, and staged multiple coups that installed or deposed presidents—including himself. Santa Anna was president of Mexico at least eleven times (though not all terms were completed), switching allegiances in pursuit of personal power.

Political Opportunism

Santa Anna's popularity stemmed partly from his independence war credentials and his knack for portraying himself as a savior during crises. Yet he often left day-to-day governance to vice-presidents or ministers while he withdrew to his hacienda in Veracruz. When political winds shifted, Santa Anna would stage another coup or issue a plan (manifesto) to justify toppling the existing regime. This "politics by pronunciamiento" became a defining feature of early Mexican public life.

17.4 REGIONAL CAUDILLOS AND PERSISTENT INSTABILITY

Caudillismo
Years of war and weak central institutions gave rise to **caudillos**—strong regional leaders who commanded loyalty through personal charisma, patronage, and military might. Figures like **Juan Álvarez** in the south or **Francisco García** in the north effectively ruled their states, often ignoring decrees from Mexico City if they clashed with local interests.

- **Militarized Politics**: Many caudillos, lacking formal political structures, settled disputes with arms. Frequent pronunciamientos (public statements calling for regime change) meant that governments rose and fell at gunpoint, paralyzing administrative continuity.

Conflicts over Church and Military Privileges
Two powerful institutions shaped regional alignments:

1. **The Church**: Conservative factions defended clerical privileges (fueros), Church landholdings, and Catholicism's monopoly. Liberals, in contrast, wanted to reduce Church influence in civil matters.
2. **The Army**: Generals or colonels saw themselves as guardians of the nation's independence, demanding privileges akin to the Church. Military fueros exempted them from civil courts, fueling resentment among civilians.

Economic Consequences
Constant coups and local strongmen undermined economic recovery. Investors hesitated to fund large projects like infrastructure or mining expansions, fearing abrupt policy shifts. The government struggled to collect taxes or repay foreign loans, compounding debt. Smuggling flourished where local caudillos turned a blind eye or profited from bribes.

17.5 ATTEMPTS AT REFORM: THE CENTRALIST PERIOD AND BACKLASH

Centralist Republic (1835–1846)
Fed up with persistent revolts, conservatives gained traction and dismantled the federal system in the 1830s, creating a **Centralist Republic** under a series of

constitutive laws known as the **Siete Leyes** (Seven Laws). These abolished state legislatures, replaced states with "departments," and concentrated authority in Mexico City.

- **Santa Anna and Centralism**: Santa Anna, now allied with conservative elites, supported centralism to curb rebellious states. But ironically, the new arrangement provoked more uprisings, as regions like Texas refused to cede local autonomy.

The Texas Revolt (1835–1836)
Among the staunchest opponents of centralism were the Anglophone settlers in **Texas**, who had immigrated under prior federalist policies that granted them local freedoms. Once centralism tightened restrictions, tensions exploded, culminating in the **Texas Revolution**. Santa Anna personally led troops north, capturing the Alamo but ultimately suffering defeat at **San Jacinto** (April 1836). Texas declared independence.

- **Legacy for Mexico**: Losing Texas emboldened other regional separatists and tarnished Santa Anna's reputation. Some Mexicans blamed the fiasco on incompetent leadership or misguided centralism. Economic woes deepened as Mexico now faced the potential fragmentation of other northern territories.

17.6 REVERTING TO FEDERALISM AND NEW CRISES

Return to Federalism
Humiliated by the Texas loss and internal rebellions, Mexico oscillated back to federalism in 1846. This was partly orchestrated by liberals who believed strong local governance would better reflect Mexico's diversity. Santa Anna, ever the opportunist, adapted once more, presenting himself as a born-again federalist if it served his comeback.

Economic and Diplomatic Anxieties

- **Mounting Foreign Debt**: Repeated loans during the independence wars, plus new ones to quell internal revolts, left Mexico heavily indebted. European creditors—particularly Britain—demanded repayments, threatening naval blockades or punitive measures if Mexico defaulted.

- **U.S. Tensions**: The United States, having annexed Texas in 1845, loomed as a growing threat. Border disputes and American expansionism foreshadowed larger conflicts. Mexico's unsettled finances and precarious governance made it vulnerable to external pressure, setting the stage for the looming U.S.-Mexican War.

Growing Ideological Divide

By the mid-1840s, liberals and conservatives had cemented distinct platforms:

- **Liberals**: Favored freedom of the press, reduced Church and military fueros, and strong local governance. Some were radical enough to propose selling Church lands to alleviate public debt.
- **Conservatives**: Argued that Mexico needed stable, centralized rule, allied with the Church and army to maintain social order. They believed liberal reforms endangered religious unity and could spark anarchy among the masses.

Despite short-lived alliances, these poles repeatedly clashed, leading to constitutional rewrites and ephemeral regimes. The brewing tensions with the U.S. over territorial claims would soon overshadow these internal debates, thrusting Mexico into a war that would profoundly reshape its future.

17.7 CULTURAL AND SOCIAL DEVELOPMENTS IN THE EARLY REPUBLIC

Literature and National Identity
The early republic saw a surge in political pamphlets, newspapers, and patriotic literature. Intellectuals debated Mexico's indigenous heritage, independence heroism, and the role of Catholic tradition in forging a cohesive nation. Writers like **José Joaquín Fernández de Lizardi** (El Pensador Mexicano) used satire to critique government corruption and champion popular enlightenment.

Art, Music, and Religious Expressions

- **Religious Festivals**: Despite calls from some liberals to curtail Church influence, religious processions and feasts remained central to local communities. The Virgin of Guadalupe continued as a national symbol, unifying diverse social groups.
- **Visual Arts**: Portraits of independence leaders and battle scenes commemorated Mexico's founding. However, ongoing turmoil limited grand cultural patronage. Artists often relied on private commissions from wealthy families or local churches.

Everyday Life and Social Stratification
For ordinary people, especially Indigenous peasants and urban poor, the early republic's ideals of liberty and citizenship often felt distant. Land inequalities persisted; wages remained low; local strongmen could oppress or protect communities at whim. Nonetheless, the period did see some free Afro-Mexican communities and mestizos gain modest upward mobility through military service or political patronage in the new republic's many armies and factions.

17.8 THE LEGACY OF THE EARLY REPUBLIC

By the mid-19th century, Mexico's experiment with republican governance had revealed deep structural weaknesses. Constant leadership changes drained resources and morale. Centralism and federalism seesawed, often overshadowing crucial questions of economic development and social reform. The Church's vast influence persisted, and the military remained a potent force in politics. While independence had freed Mexico from Spanish rule, the country found itself grappling with a new set of challenges: defining a cohesive national project, managing foreign debts, reconciling liberal and conservative visions, and preserving territorial integrity in the face of expansionist neighbors.

Heading into the next phase of its history, Mexico would confront external threats—particularly from the United States—that would drastically reshape its borders and fuel internal strife. The next chapter examines these **foreign interventions**, revealing how wars with major powers tested Mexico's survival and laid the groundwork for subsequent transformations in national identity and governance.

CHAPTER 18

FOREIGN INTERVENTIONS (MID-19TH CENTURY)

Mexico's early republic was fraught with instability, leaving it vulnerable to encroachment by stronger foreign nations. The mid-19th century saw multiple conflicts in which Mexico lost significant territory or faced invasive military occupations. The most notable of these involved the **United States**—culminating in the Mexican-American War—and later **European powers** under the banner of the so-called "French Intervention." These events tested Mexico's resilience, prompting shifts in leadership, spurring new constitutional reforms, and forging nationalist sentiments that would shape the country's modern identity. This chapter chronicles those pivotal foreign incursions, from the annexation of Texas to the ephemeral French-imposed monarchy of Maximilian.

18.1 THE ROAD TO THE MEXICAN-AMERICAN WAR

Annexation of Texas (1845)
The rift between Mexico and the United States over **Texas** deepened after the region declared independence in 1836 and subsequently sought American annexation. Despite Mexican protests, the U.S. Congress ratified annexation in December 1845, viewing Texas as part of its "manifest destiny" to expand across North America. For Mexico—still refusing to recognize Texan independence—this was tantamount to a declaration of hostility.

Border Disputes and Diplomatic Failures

- **Nueces vs. Rio Grande**: Mexico maintained that Texas ended at the Nueces River, while the U.S. insisted the border lay farther south at the Rio Grande. This dispute left a swath of contested territory.
- **Diplomatic Missions**: President **James K. Polk** offered to buy California and New Mexico territories, but Mexican leaders—amid political chaos—rebuffed the approach. Meanwhile, a U.S. army under General **Zachary Taylor** moved into the disputed zone, escalating tensions.

Outbreak of War (1846)
In April 1846, a skirmish between Mexican and American troops near the Rio Grande offered Polk grounds to claim Mexico had "shed American blood on

American soil." The U.S. Congress declared war in May. Many Americans enthusiastically supported the war, while others, notably northern abolitionists, criticized it as an attempt to expand slave-holding states. Mexico, burdened by internal strife, braced for a difficult defense.

18.2 KEY CAMPAIGNS OF THE MEXICAN-AMERICAN WAR

Northern Front: Taylor and Santa Anna

General Zachary Taylor advanced from Texas into northern Mexico, capturing Monterrey (1846) after fierce resistance. Santa Anna, having reemerged in Mexican politics, tried to rally an army but faced shortages of funds and supplies. Though Santa Anna's forces fought bravely at **Buena Vista** (February 1847), they ultimately retreated, allowing Taylor to secure control of key northern strongholds.

Pacific and Western Fronts

Meanwhile, U.S. forces and settlers in California's "Bear Flag Revolt" overthrew the minimal Mexican presence. The U.S. Navy seized ports along the Pacific coast, effectively cutting off Mexico's maritime trade routes. In New Mexico, another contingent faced little opposition, as local power brokers weighed shifting allegiances.

Central Campaign: Scott's March to Mexico City

A decisive blow came from the Gulf Coast: General **Winfield Scott** landed near Veracruz in March 1847, laid siege to the port, and then advanced inland along the route Hernán Cortés once took. After victories at **Cerro Gordo**, **Churubusco**, and **Chapultepec**, U.S. troops entered **Mexico City** in September 1847, marking a stunning humiliation for Mexican defenders. The capital's fall clinched the war.

18.3 THE TREATY OF GUADALUPE HIDALGO AND ITS CONSEQUENCES

Treaty Provisions (1848)
Defeated and occupied, Mexico was compelled to sign the **Treaty of Guadalupe Hidalgo** in February 1848. The agreement forced Mexico to cede:

1. **California**
2. **New Mexico**
3. **Arizona**
4. **Nevada**
5. Parts of **Colorado** and **Utah**

The U.S. pledged to pay Mexico $15 million in compensation—far below the territories' long-term value—and to assume some Mexican debts to U.S. citizens. This vast territorial transfer, amounting to nearly half of Mexico's pre-war land, remains one of the largest in modern history.

National Trauma
For Mexicans, the loss of territory was a profound national trauma. Political factions blamed each other or Santa Anna's leadership. Some argued that internal divisions had weakened the country against foreign aggression. Moreover, the war reinforced a sense of wounded pride and spurred calls for drastic reforms to rebuild a stronger, more unified state.

Enduring Effects

- **Geopolitical Shift**: The U.S. emerged with a continental reach, while Mexico found its northern frontier drastically redrawn.
- **Economic Wounds**: Rebuilding war-torn infrastructure demanded resources Mexico lacked, deepening reliance on foreign loans.
- **Military and Political Upheaval**: Santa Anna's regime collapsed; new liberal forces sought to transform Mexico's institutions, culminating in the era of **La Reforma**.

18.4 POST-WAR STRUGGLES AND THE ERA OF LA REFORMA

Santa Anna's Final Governments
In the wake of defeat, Santa Anna returned to power repeatedly, but public disillusionment soared. He sold more territory—the **Gadsden Purchase**

(1853)—to the U.S. for $10 million, hoping to bolster finances. However, the move outraged nationalists. Meanwhile, conspiracies flourished. By 1855, liberal generals ousted Santa Anna, ushering in a profound attempt to reshape Mexico: the **Reform**.

La Reforma (1855–1861)
Under liberal leaders like **Benito Juárez**, **Miguel Lerdo de Tejada**, and **Melchor Ocampo**, a new generation sought to curb military and ecclesiastical privileges, modernize legal codes, and stimulate economic growth. Key measures included:

- **Lerdo Law (1856)**: Mandating the sale of communal (Church and Indigenous) lands to encourage private property.
- **Juárez Law**: Abolishing special fueros for clergy and military, placing all citizens under common civil courts.
- **Constitution of 1857**: Enshrining individual rights, freedom of speech, and secular education, though Catholicism remained predominant culturally.

Conservative Backlash
Threatening the Church's wealth and the army's status triggered fierce conservative opposition. These reforms split the country, igniting the **War of the Reform** (1858–1861)—a civil war pitting liberal and conservative governments against each other. Liberals eventually triumphed, installing Juárez in Mexico City and consolidating a more secular, progressive agenda. But the victory was brief; foreign powers, alarmed by Mexico's debt defaults, soon intervened, thrusting the nation into a new crisis.

18.5 THE FRENCH INTERVENTION AND MAXIMILIAN'S EMPIRE

European Intrusion
By 1861, Mexico's finances were once again in disarray. Juárez suspended foreign debt payments. In response, Britain, Spain, and France formed a coalition to demand repayment. While Britain and Spain withdrew after negotiations, France—under **Emperor Napoleon III**—had grander ambitions: establishing a friendly monarchy in Mexico to expand French influence.

The French Invasion (1862)
French troops landed at Veracruz, marching inland. Mexican forces, though exhausted from the Reform War, put up stiff resistance. On **May 5, 1862**, General **Ignacio Zaragoza** achieved an unexpected victory at the **Battle of Puebla**,

momentarily halting the French. This success is commemorated as **Cinco de Mayo**, a potent symbol of national pride. Yet the French soon regrouped with reinforcements.

Installment of Maximilian
By 1863, the French captured Mexico City. Conservatives welcomed them, hoping foreign backing would crush liberal reforms. Napoleon III offered the crown to **Archduke Maximilian of Habsburg**, who arrived in 1864 with his wife **Carlota**. Proclaiming the **Second Mexican Empire**, Maximilian introduced some liberal-leaning policies—like respecting certain aspects of the Juárez Constitution—but relied on French bayonets and conservative supporters.

18.6 REPUBLICAN RESISTANCE UNDER JUÁREZ

Government-in-Exile
Benito Juárez, refusing to recognize Maximilian, set up a "republican government on the move" in northern Mexico, communicating with governors and generals still loyal to the constitution. Despite limited resources, they sustained guerrilla warfare and diplomatic efforts—seeking U.S. moral support, especially after the American Civil War ended.

Declining French Support
When the U.S. Civil War concluded in 1865, the newly unified United States demanded France withdraw under the Monroe Doctrine, which opposed European interference in the Americas. Napoleon III, facing domestic criticism and new European complications, gradually reduced his Mexican expeditionary forces. Maximilian, isolated and lacking funds, struggled to maintain control beyond central regions.

Victory for the Republic (1867)
By early 1867, liberal republican forces—led by **Generals Mariano Escobedo** and **Porfirio Díaz**—recaptured major cities. Maximilian's last stand was in Querétaro, where he surrendered in May. A court-martial sentenced him to death. Despite pleas for clemency from European monarchs, Juárez upheld the verdict, and Maximilian was executed in June 1867. The ephemeral empire collapsed, and Juárez reentered Mexico City as a triumphant symbol of national sovereignty.

18.7 AFTERMATH AND REBUILDING

Reassertion of Liberal Reforms
With the monarchy ended, Juárez and his allies reaffirmed the 1857 Constitution, continuing measures to secularize the nation, limit the Church's privileges, and modernize the legal system. Infrastructure projects, though constrained by debt, gained impetus as Mexico tried to catch up with global industrial trends.

Rise of Porfirio Díaz
A hero of the republican victory, **Porfirio Díaz** soon emerged as a key military figure and political contender. While Juárez and his successor, **Sebastián Lerdo de Tejada**, worked to strengthen federal institutions, Díaz developed a loyal following. He would eventually seize power in 1876, inaugurating a new epoch often called the **Porfiriato**—marked by authoritarian stability, foreign investment, and modernization, but also deep social inequalities.

Legacy of Foreign Interventions
The mid-19th century's wars with the United States and France left an indelible mark on Mexico. Although humiliating in many respects—costing territories and imposing foreign rulers—these trials forged a stronger sense of national identity and underscored the need for internal unity. Leaders like Juárez became national icons, celebrated for defending sovereignty and liberal principles against external foes. At the same time, lasting scars—territorial loss, economic debts, and internal rifts—would challenge Mexico's future development.

18.8 SIGNIFICANCE OF THE MID-19TH-CENTURY INTERVENTIONS

By the late 1860s, Mexico had overcome two major foreign invasions—first by the United States and then by France. These conflicts shaped national consciousness, revealing both the fragility of Mexico's young institutions and the resilience of its people when confronting foreign aggression. The loss of northern territories to the United States starkly demonstrated the price of internal discord, while the defeat of Maximilian's French-backed empire showcased Mexico's capacity to rally around republican ideals. Yet internal power struggles did not disappear; they merely evolved. The next decades would see the ascendancy of Porfirio Díaz, the consolidation of a new authoritarian order, and tensions that would erupt again in a revolutionary wave early in the 20th century.

In the chapters ahead, we explore how Mexico navigated the post-intervention era: forging industrial changes, attracting foreign capital, and confronting the social inequalities that eventually sparked the Mexican Revolution—one of the defining upheavals of the modern world.

CHAPTER 19

THE ROAD TO THE REVOLUTION (1876 – 1910)

By the late 19th century, Mexico emerged from a tumultuous era of foreign invasions and civil strife only to be shaped by the dominant figure of **Porfirio Díaz**. Seizing power in 1876, Díaz consolidated control and ushered in a period of relative stability and modernization often called the **Porfiriato**. While his regime advanced railroads, mining, and foreign investment, it also deepened social inequalities, suppressed political dissent, and dispossessed peasants of communal lands. Over time, the strains of authoritarian rule and economic dislocation set the stage for a widespread revolt. This chapter examines the long lead-up to the Mexican Revolution: the structure of the Porfirian regime, its economic policies, social consequences, and the growing undercurrent of discontent that would explode by 1910.

19.1 THE RISE OF PORFIRIO DÍAZ

Background and Early Coup
Porfirio Díaz, a veteran of the War of the Reform and the fight against French occupation, distinguished himself as a skilled general. In 1876, he overthrew President **Sebastián Lerdo de Tejada** under the banner of the **Plan de Tuxtepec**, accusing Lerdo of seeking re-election and violating constitutional principles. This coup propelled Díaz to the presidency. Over the ensuing decades, he fashioned a centralized political machine that suppressed local strongmen, manipulated elections, and used patronage networks to maintain power.

"Pan o Palo"
A telling phrase of the Porfiriato was **"Pan o Palo"** ("bread or the stick"), signifying how Díaz dealt with allies and opponents:

- **Pan (Bread):** Rewards for supporters, such as government posts, concessions, or protection for business ventures. Many local caciques, military officers, and intellectuals found personal advancement by allying with Díaz.

- **Palo (Stick)**: Repression of dissent. Political rivals were exiled, imprisoned, or marginalized. Indigenous and peasant uprisings were brutally put down. Newspapers criticizing the regime faced censorship or closure.

Limited Democracy and the Circle of Científicos

Although Mexico nominally held elections, these were stage-managed affairs ensuring Díaz's continuous re-elections. He occasionally placed a trusted ally—like **Manuel González**—in the presidency (1880-1884) to present a veneer of constitutional rule, but always returned to dominate the political arena.

- **Científicos**: A coterie of technocratic advisors known as the **Científicos** guided Díaz's economic and social policies. Influenced by positivism (Auguste Comte's philosophy championing science and order), they believed in "scientific governance" by an enlightened elite. Figures like **Justo Sierra**, **José Yves Limantour**, and **Rosalío Martínez** shaped policies on finance, education, and infrastructure, rationalizing authoritarian controls as necessary for progress.

19.2 PORFIRIAN ECONOMICS AND MODERNIZATION

Railroad Boom

One of the most visible achievements of the Porfiriato was the dramatic expansion of Mexico's railway network:

- **Foreign Investment**: Diaz's regime attracted British and U.S. capital to build rail lines connecting distant states to Mexico City and ports on the Gulf and Pacific. Investors received generous concessions, including land grants and tax exemptions.
- **Economic Integration**: By linking mining centers, agricultural zones, and urban markets, railroads spurred trade and quickened industrialization in major cities. A national market began forming, and goods like minerals, henequen, sugar, and coffee could reach foreign buyers more efficiently.

Mining and Foreign Concessions

Miners discovered new silver lodes, while copper, lead, and other minerals became lucrative exports. Major U.S. companies—like the Guggenheim interests—acquired large-scale operations. Díaz's administration welcomed these investors, granting them favorable terms and, in practice, allowing them to exert significant influence over local labor conditions.

Agribusiness and Land Concentration
An insatiable demand for export crops—sugar, henequen (for rope), coffee, and later rubber—led to:

- **Haciendas Expansion**: Wealthy landowners and foreign syndicates acquired massive estates, often absorbing communal lands through legal loopholes. Under the 1856 Lerdo Law and subsequent reforms, the regime encouraged private property, disbanding many Indigenous ejidos (communal land holdings).
- **Peasant Displacement**: Indigenous and mestizo smallholders found themselves dispossessed, forced into wage labor or debt peonage on these giant estates. This widespread loss of land sowed deep resentment.

Urban Growth and Social Divide
While the Porfiriato spurred modernization, it also accentuated socio-economic gaps:

- **Cosmopolitan Elite**: A class of affluent landowners, industrialists, and officials enjoyed European luxuries, fine mansions, and cultural sophistication. Mexico City, Guadalajara, and Monterrey reflected this wealth in neoclassical public buildings and flourishing cafés.
- **Rural Poverty and Urban Slums**: In contrast, the majority of peasants and laborers faced meager wages. In newly industrializing hubs, low-income workers crowded into squalid tenements lacking basic services. Rural unrest simmered beneath the outward façade of growth.

19.3 POLITICAL CONTROL AND THE "PEACE OF PORFIRIO"

Authoritarian Stability
Díaz prided himself on imposing "order and progress." Through a network of jefes políticos (local political bosses), he suppressed banditry and rebellious caciques. Newspapers praising the regime received subsidies, while critical journalists faced intimidation. Political clubs and opposition parties seldom lasted; each election cycle reaffirmed Díaz's victory.

The Rural Police Force (Rurales)
To maintain rural peace, Díaz expanded the **Rurales**, a mounted police corps known for swift, often brutal tactics against highway robbers or rebellious peasants. Their presence facilitated the safe transport of goods and showcased the regime's commitment to law and order. However, the Rurales frequently acted with impunity, fueling resentment in neglected provinces.

The Role of the Church
While officially a liberal state (the Reform Laws remained in effect), Díaz pursued a pragmatic approach with the Catholic Church. He allowed a partial revival of clerical influence, especially in education and charitable works, as long as the Church did not openly challenge his authority. This tacit alliance with conservative elites helped stabilize his rule in deeply Catholic regions, though anti-clerical liberals criticized these compromises.

19.4 OPPOSITION VOICES AND EARLY CRACKS

Local Uprisings and Labor Strikes
Beneath the calm surface, sporadic revolts occurred, often localized and quickly crushed:

- **Indigenous Rebellions**: For instance, the Yaqui in Sonora resisted dispossession of their ancestral lands. Díaz's forces relocated thousands of Yaquis to plantations in Yucatán, essentially enslaving them.
- **Workers' Agitation**: In industrial and mining towns, discontent over low wages, dangerous conditions, and company stores sparked strikes. A notable example was the **Cananea strike** (1906) in Sonora's copper mines, suppressed with the help of U.S. rangers. These conflicts showcased emerging class consciousness among laborers.

The Flores Magón Brothers

Ricardo and **Enrique Flores Magón**, radical journalists and intellectuals, launched the newspaper **Regeneración**, critiquing Porfirian injustices—particularly the dispossession of peasants and brutal labor conditions. Exiled to the United States, they continued to distribute clandestine pamphlets calling for overthrow of Díaz and advocating anarchist-tinged reforms. Though small in following at first, their ideas galvanized a segment of Mexico's oppressed classes and planted seeds for future revolutionary currents.

Discontent Among the Middle Class

A growing **middle class**—shopkeepers, teachers, minor bureaucrats—began questioning the lack of political freedoms. Many believed Mexico had outgrown dictatorial rule and yearned for real elections. They viewed Díaz's advanced age and the heavy-handed rule of his circle (the Científicos) as an obstacle to further economic development or social modernization. Intellectuals lamented the intellectual stagnation caused by censorship, and activists demanded space for free debate.

19.5 EMERGENCE OF FRANCISCO I. MADERO AND POLITICAL REFORM MOVEMENTS

The Díaz-Creelman Interview (1908)

In a surprising twist, Díaz granted an interview to U.S. journalist **James Creelman** in 1908, declaring he would welcome an opposition party and would not seek re-election in 1910. Some speculated Díaz was testing the waters, seeking to ensure a peaceful transition by handpicking a successor. Regardless, many took Díaz's statement seriously, seeing an opening to push for democratic reforms.

Francisco I. Madero

An unlikely figure emerged: **Francisco I. Madero**, a wealthy hacendado from Coahuila, deeply influenced by liberal ideals. Madero wrote **La sucesión presidencial en 1910**, accusing Díaz's regime of stifling true democracy and calling for honest elections. Although Madero did not advocate radical social changes at first, his emphasis on political rights electrified middle-class and some working-class audiences, who saw him as a genuine alternative to permanent Porfirian rule.

Anticipating the 1910 Elections

Inspired by Madero's calls, clubs formed to back his candidacy. Alarmed by Madero's rising popularity, Díaz reneged on his earlier statements, deciding to run again. In a familiar pattern, police harassed Madero supporters, seized newspapers, and eventually jailed Madero. This heightened the sense that Díaz had no intention of leaving office voluntarily, fanning discontent across diverse sectors—liberal intellectuals, peasants seeking land restoration, miners, and laborers demanding better wages.

19.6 THE BREAKING POINT: THE 1910 ELECTION AND CALL TO ARMS

Fraudulent Election

True to form, Díaz manipulated the 1910 presidential race. Madero, released on bail, fled to the United States. With no serious challenger, Díaz secured another term. Many previously apathetic citizens saw the blatant fraud as a final betrayal. The younger generation especially resented the octogenarian president's refusal to relinquish control.

Plan of San Luis Potosí

While in exile in San Antonio, Texas, Madero drafted the **Plan of San Luis Potosí**, which he dated retroactively to October 5, 1910, in the city of San Luis Potosí to symbolize continuity with Mexico. The plan declared the recent elections invalid, proclaimed Madero as provisional president, and called for an armed uprising on **November 20, 1910**, to overthrow Díaz.

- **Promise of Land Reform**: Initially mild in earlier writings, Madero's plan hinted at returning lands unfairly taken from peasants, appealing to the dispossessed. This promise would later be elaborated by other revolutionary leaders.

Diverse Factions Answer the Call

Though Madero's exact pronouncement had moderate language, various groups interpreted it to match their aspirations:

- **Northern Ranchers and Outlaws**: Figures like **Pancho Villa** in Chihuahua saw an opportunity for both personal advancement and social justice.
- **Southern Peasants**: Led by **Emiliano Zapata** in Morelos, they demanded the restitution of communal lands.
- **Middle-Class Liberals**: Urban professionals viewed Madero's uprising as a chance to establish democratic rule.

The stage was set for a complex, multi-faceted rebellion that would soon evolve into the **Mexican Revolution**—a prolonged conflict that would transform Mexico's institutions, social relations, and national identity for decades to come.

19.7 LEGACIES OF THE PORFIRIATO AND THE ROAD TO REVOLUTION

When Porfirio Díaz seized power in 1876, his regime brought relative stability and industrial growth, but at steep social cost. The concentration of land and wealth, alongside the suppression of political freedoms, embittered peasants, workers, and intellectuals alike. Over thirty years, discontents multiplied, intensifying as Díaz extended his rule far beyond initial promises. By 1910, many Mexicans saw no peaceful route to reform.

- **Economic Modernization**: Railways and foreign investments undeniably modernized parts of Mexico, but wages for laborers remained stagnant, and rural communities lost ancestral lands.
- **Social Tensions**: Middle-class grievances about political exclusion, combined with the radicalization of laborers and peasants, formed a broad coalition for revolt.
- **Political Rigidities**: Díaz's authoritarian approach left no avenue for gradual reform or leadership renewal, making a violent rupture almost inevitable.

In the next chapter, we delve into the Revolution itself—how Madero's call ignited various regional uprisings, the emergence of formidable leaders such as Villa and Zapata, and the eventual drafting of a new constitution that sought to remake Mexico's social and political frameworks. While independence had freed Mexico from Spain, the Revolution sought to free Mexico from internal autocracy and reshape it in the image of social justice and democracy.

CHAPTER 20

THE MEXICAN REVOLUTION AND ITS AFTERMATH (1910 – 1940)

The Mexican Revolution (1910–1920) stands as one of the most defining and transformative upheavals in modern Latin American history. Sparked by widespread anger at the aging Porfirio Díaz regime, the revolution evolved into a sprawling, multi-sided conflict featuring charismatic leaders such as **Francisco I. Madero, Pancho Villa, Emiliano Zapata,** and **Venustiano Carranza**. Revolving around demands for land, labor rights, and political freedoms, the decade of turmoil ended in the creation of the **Constitution of 1917**, a groundbreaking charter that promised sweeping reforms. Yet the path to lasting stability proved arduous. This chapter examines the Revolution's phases, the key personalities, the ideological divides, and the contested process of rebuilding Mexico in the aftermath.

20.1 THE MADERO REVOLUTION (1910 – 1911)

Initial Uprisings and Díaz's Downfall

Following the **Plan of San Luis Potosí**, pockets of rebellion flared in northern Mexico under figures like **Francisco "Pancho" Villa** and **Pascual Orozco**, while in the south, **Emiliano Zapata** led peasants demanding **"Tierra y Libertad"** (Land and Liberty). Under pressure from multiple fronts:

- **Ciudad Juárez** fell to rebel forces in May 1911, a symbolic victory that convinced Díaz to negotiate.
- Díaz resigned shortly thereafter, exiling himself to France. Madero entered triumphantly, championed as the apostle of democracy.

Madero's Presidency

Elected president in late 1911, Madero aimed to establish liberal democracy—free press, fair elections, some land reform. However, he faced immediate challenges:

1. **Old Porfirian Holdovers**: Many Díaz loyalists remained in the army, judiciary, and bureaucracy, resisting Madero's authority or plotting against him.

2. **Zapata's Disappointment**: Zapata believed Madero moved too slowly on agrarian reform, issuing the **Plan of Ayala (1911)**, denouncing Madero as betraying peasants.
3. **Rising Discontent**: Northern warlords like Orozco, who had expected high office or quick social reforms, also turned against Madero.

Eroding Support
Attempts at moderate compromise satisfied neither the conservative elites nor the radical grassroots. Rebellions broke out, overshadowing Madero's democratic initiatives. The federal army proved reluctant to defend him wholeheartedly, led by generals still loyal to Porfirian ideals. By 1913, the stage was set for a counter-revolutionary strike.

20.2 THE TRAGIC TEN DAYS AND HUERTA'S DICTATORSHIP

La Decena Trágica (Ten Tragic Days)
In February 1913, a coup erupted in Mexico City. Two rebel generals—**Félix Díaz** (nephew of Porfirio) and **Bernardo Reyes**—led troops against Madero. For ten days, the capital became a battlefield, with artillery shells striking the city center. Ambiguously, the sitting army chief, **General Victoriano Huerta**, was supposed to defend Madero but instead colluded with the rebels.

Madero's Murder
After a brief standoff, Huerta betrayed Madero, arresting him and Vice President **José María Pino Suárez**. Claiming to "restore order," Huerta seized the presidency. Days later, Madero and Pino Suárez were assassinated while allegedly "attempting to escape." The shocking double murder outraged the revolutionary factions, who saw Huerta as a traitor.

Huerta's Regime (1913–1914)
Huerta reinstated Porfirian tactics—centralizing power, suppressing dissent, and courting conservative landowners and the Church. He reestablished ties with foreign businesses eager for stability. But the outrages of the coup galvanized revolutionaries:

- **Carranza's Constitutionalist Army**: **Venustiano Carranza**, governor of Coahuila, declared Huerta illegitimate, rallying northern states to form a "Constitutionalist" movement.

- **Villa and Zapata**: Furious at Madero's betrayal, they too refused to recognize Huerta, mustering their own local militias to fight the new dictatorship.

20.3 THE CONSTITUTIONALIST VICTORY AND INTERNAL DIVISIONS

Northern Advances

Carranza, styling himself as the "Primer Jefe" (First Chief) of the Constitutionalist Army, coordinated with generals like **Álvaro Obregón** in Sonora and **Pancho Villa** in Chihuahua. Their well-organized campaigns hammered Huerta's federal forces.

- **Villa's División del Norte**: Noted for cavalry raids and popular support among ranchers and peasants, Villa's army secured large swathes of northern territory.
- **Obregón's Military Skill**: A methodical strategist, Obregón used trench warfare and modern tactics, outmaneuvering Huerta's troops in key battles.

Huerta's Fall and Exile

By mid-1914, Constitutionalists converged on the capital. International pressures—especially from the U.S. government under President **Woodrow Wilson**, which refused to recognize Huerta—further weakened the dictatorship. Huerta resigned in July 1914 and fled. Carranza entered Mexico City soon after, claiming leadership of a provisional government.

A Splintered Alliance

Though united against Huerta, Constitutionalist leaders held divergent goals. Villa, Zapata, and Obregón each possessed distinct power bases. Carranza, emphasizing legal continuity, declared himself the rightful head of state. Villa and Zapata favored more radical social reforms—immediate land redistribution, worker rights, and local autonomy. Tensions erupted when Carranza resisted or delayed implementing such changes.

20.4 CIVIL WAR AMONG REVOLUTIONARIES (1914 – 1915)

Convention of Aguascalientes

Hoping to reconcile differences, revolutionary generals convened in Aguascalientes (late 1914). The assembly recognized **Eulalio Gutiérrez** as interim president, marginalizing Carranza. Villa and Zapata allied, entering Mexico City and demanding sweeping reforms. However, the "Conventionist" alliance lacked a unified strategy.

Carranza and Obregón vs. Villa and Zapata

Carranza, refusing to cede authority, retreated to Veracruz and reorganized forces with Obregón. The resulting conflict pitted:

- **División del Norte** (Villa) and the **Zapatistas** in Morelos
- **Carrancistas** led by Obregón's disciplined army
  While Zapata's peasant fighters held their own in southern strongholds, Villa's cavalry struggled against Obregón's modern tactics. Obregón, employing trench warfare and machine guns, inflicted major defeats on Villa in battles like **Celaya** (April 1915). By late 1915, Villa's power ebbed, and Zapata remained largely contained in Morelos.

Violence and Social Upheaval

The war's scale was unprecedented, claiming hundreds of thousands of lives through combat, disease, and famine. Rail lines were destroyed, farmland neglected, and towns frequently changed hands. Civilians bore the brunt, facing forced conscription or extortion by roving armies. Nonetheless, each faction championed populist rhetoric—Zapata's "Tierra y Libertad," Villa's flamboyant outlaw heroism, and Carranza's calls for constitutional order—reflecting the Revolution's complexity as both a power struggle and a social uprising.

20.5 THE CONSTITUTION OF 1917 AND RADICAL REFORMS

Carranza's Ascendancy

By 1916, Carranza consolidated the northern states and gained U.S. diplomatic recognition, further isolating Villa and Zapata. In December 1916, he convened a constitutional congress in Querétaro, urging delegates to craft a new charter reflecting revolutionary principles.

- **Obregón's Influence**: Although absent from the congress, Obregón's alignment with Carranza meant moderate yet progressive reforms were on the table—tempered by concerns about not alienating the middle classes or foreign investors.

Key Articles

The **Constitution of 1917**, promulgated on February 5, stands as one of the most advanced of its time:

- **Article 3**: Secular, free primary education, stripping the Church of control over public schooling.
- **Article 27**: Declared land and subsoil resources property of the nation, paving the way for agrarian reform and nationalization of mineral or oil wealth.
- **Article 123**: Enshrined labor rights—eight-hour workday, right to strike, equal pay, wage protections. This article was groundbreaking, giving Mexico some of the earliest labor protections in the world.
- **Article 130**: Restricted the Church's role in civil matters, continuing the anti-clerical stance from earlier liberal reforms.

Significance

The 1917 Constitution codified much of the Revolution's social aspirations. Yet implementing these radical provisions would take decades, as entrenched elites, foreign corporations, and moderate revolutionaries sought to limit or roll back the more leftist elements.

20.6 FACTIONS, BETRAYALS, AND THE END OF THE MAJOR VIOLENCE

Demise of Zapata (1919)

Despite the Constitution's promise of agrarian reform, Emiliano Zapata saw little progress in Morelos. In 1919, Zapata was lured into an ambush by a Carrancista officer, **Jesús Guajardo**, and assassinated. His death ended the most powerful grassroots movement for peasant autonomy. Though lamented by many, the institutionalizing revolution pressed on without him.

Villa's Capitulation

Villa continued guerrilla attacks in the north, even raiding Columbus, New Mexico (1916) and provoking a U.S. expedition into Mexican territory. By 1920, exhausted and isolated, he negotiated an amnesty with the post-Carranza government (now led by interim President Adolfo de la Huerta) and retired to a hacienda. Like Zapata, he was later assassinated (1923), reflecting the regime's desire to neutralize disruptive warlords.

The Overthrow of Carranza (1920)

Carranza's presidency ended in betrayal similar to Madero's fate. As his term expired, Carranza favored a civilian successor over the popular general Álvaro

Obregón. Obregón rebelled with other generals, forcing Carranza to flee Mexico City. Carranza was killed en route, and Obregón took the presidency. This concluded the era of the Great Caudillos—Madero, Huerta, Villa, Zapata, Carranza—each had died violently. Obregón emerged as the revolution's new arbiter, focusing on institutional rebuilding.

20.7 REBUILDING THE NATION: OBREGÓN, CALLES, AND THE INSTITUTIONALIZATION

Obregón's Presidency (1920–1924)

As president, **Álvaro Obregón** sought to implement moderate social reforms while reassuring foreign investors. Key initiatives included:

- **Labor Alliances**: He courted the **Confederación Regional Obrera Mexicana** (CROM), a major labor union, and facilitated some worker-friendly policies.
- **Education under José Vasconcelos**: Vasconcelos spearheaded a cultural renaissance, launching literacy campaigns, rural schools, and murals by artists like **Diego Rivera**, **José Clemente Orozco**, and **David Alfaro Siqueiros**.

Plutarco Elías Calles and the Maximato

Obregón's successor, **Plutarco Elías Calles** (1924–1928), advanced the formation of a state apparatus that regulated labor, brokered with foreign oil companies, and suppressed Catholic resistance (the **Cristero War**, 1926–1929). After Obregón's assassination in 1928, Calles became Mexico's de facto power broker—nicknamed **Jefe Máximo**—through puppet presidents until 1934. This period of top-down control, known as the **Maximato**, aimed to ensure revolutionary tenets survived while tamping down radical activism.

The Formation of the PNR

In 1929, Calles orchestrated the **Partido Nacional Revolucionario (PNR)**, a forerunner to the **PRI** (Institutional Revolutionary Party), consolidating revolutionary factions under a unified banner. The PNR (later rebranded PRM, and eventually PRI) became Mexico's ruling institution for much of the 20th century, mediating between workers, peasants, and an evolving middle class. This new political framework aimed to avoid another wave of caudillo violence by channeling power through structured party mechanisms.

20.8 LONG-TERM IMPACTS OF THE REVOLUTION

Agrarian Reform and Peasant Rights
Though slow and often incomplete, land redistribution advanced under subsequent administrations, especially under **Lázaro Cárdenas** (1934–1940). Ejidos were reestablished, granting communal holdings to peasants reminiscent of Zapata's demands. However, structural inequalities persisted, and corruption sometimes undermined the reforms' potential.

Labor Laws and National Identity
Article 123's labor protections laid the groundwork for union activism. The Revolution also inspired a cultural renaissance that celebrated Indigenous roots, rural life, and mestizo heritage—manifested in muralism, new literature, and nationalist music. A distinct modern Mexican identity emerged, proud of revolutionary accomplishments while conscious of unfulfilled social promises.

Church-State Relations
The anticlerical stance embedded in the 1917 Constitution triggered persistent tensions, culminating in the **Cristero War**. Over time, pragmatic accommodations arose, but the formal separation of Church and State remained a hallmark of post-revolutionary governance, forging a secular public sphere.

National vs. Foreign Interests
The Constitution's emphasis on national ownership of subsoil resources eventually paved the way for major expropriations—most famously in the **oil nationalization** of 1938 under President Cárdenas. Foreign investors complained, but these policies sought to fulfill revolutionary ideals of economic sovereignty. Mexico negotiated compensation deals that balanced anti-imperialist sentiment with pragmatic diplomacy.

20.9 CONCLUSION: A REVOLUTION'S UNFINISHED AGENDA

The Mexican Revolution dismantled the old Porfirian order and gave rise to a new constitutional framework championing social and economic rights. It also ushered in an extended period of institutional consolidation, culminating in the powerful **PRI** regime that, for better or worse, shaped Mexico's 20th-century trajectory. Although many revolutionary ideals—agrarian justice, worker empowerment, indigenous autonomy—remained partially realized, the Revolution undeniably transformed Mexico's political culture, granting broader citizenship, fostering national integration, and embedding social reforms in law.

By 1940, the nation had stabilized relative to the upheavals of the preceding decades. Presidents like Cárdenas embodied the Revolution's progressive wing, while others tilted more conservative. Still, the legacy of 1910–1920 cast a long shadow: revolutionary heroes became national symbols, the Constitution remained central to political discourse, and ongoing debates about democracy, land, labor, and the distribution of wealth carried the spirit of the Revolution into modern times. The chapters of Mexican history after 1940 would be deeply influenced by these revolutionary roots, as Mexico continued to navigate modernization, social change, and the challenges of global politics as a sovereign nation forging its own path.

Help Us Share Your Thoughts!

Dear reader,

Thank you for spending your time with this book. We hope it brought you enjoyment and a few new ideas to think about. If there was anything that didn't work for you, or if you have suggestions on how we can improve, please let us know at **kontakt@skriuwer.com**. Your feedback means a lot to us and helps us make our books even better.

If you enjoyed this book, we would be very grateful if you left a review on the site where you purchased it. Your review not only helps other readers find our books, but also encourages us to keep creating more stories and materials that you'll love.

By choosing Skriuwer, you're also supporting **Frisian**—a minority language mainly spoken in the northern Netherlands. Although **Frisian** has a rich history, the number of speakers is shrinking, and it's at risk of dying out. Your purchase helps fund resources to preserve and promote this language, such as educational programs and learning tools. If you'd like to learn more about Frisian or even start learning it yourself, please visit **www.learnfrisian.com**.

Thank you for being part of our community. We look forward to sharing more books with you in the future.

Warm regards,
The Skriuwer Team